THE ULTIMATE
COOKING FOR TWO
COOKBOOK

MR. FOOD TEST KITCHEN, MR. FOOD TEST KITCHEN oval logo, and OOH IT'S SO GOOD!!, are trademarks or registered trademarks owned by Ginsburg Enterprises Incorporated and used with permission. All Rights Reserved.

The paper in this printing meets the requirements of the ANSI Standard Z39.48-1992.

While every care has been taken in compiling the recipes for this book, the publisher, Cogin, Inc., or any other person who has been involved in working on this publication assumes no responsibility or liability for any errors or omissions, inadvertent or not, that may be found in the recipes or text, nor for any problems or damages that may arise as a result of preparing these recipes.

If food allergies or dietary restrictions are a concern, it is recommended that you carefully read ingredient product labels as well as consult a nutritionist or your physician to determine if a particular recipe meets your dietary needs.

We encourage you to use caution when working with all kitchen equipment and to always follow food safety guidelines.

To purchase this book for business or promotional use or to purchase more than 50 copies at a discount, or for custom editions, please contact Cogin, Inc. at the address below or info@mrfood.com.

Inquiries should be addressed to:
Cogin, Inc.
1770 NW 64 Street, Suite 500
Fort Lauderdale, FL 33309

ISBN: 978-0-9911934-6-2

Printed in the United States of America
First Edition

www.MrFood.com
www.EverydayDiabeticRecipes.com

Introduction

After years of providing you with thousands of recipes meant to feed your family, your friends, your neighbors, and your neighbors' neighbors, we finally decided to focus on a book that's just for two – that's you and someone lucky enough to have you in their life. It wasn't until we started working on this book that we realized how much time and money a book like this can save anyone who's cooking just for two. (Why did we wait so long?!) And, as you've come to expect from the Mr. Food Test Kitchen, all of the recipes are triple-tested for ease and taste, which means this book is jam-packed with all kinds of goodness.

For those of you who may be thinking, "Why would I need a cookbook for two? Why not just cut a recipe in half, or thirds?" Well, before you start taking out your calculators, it's not that simple! We learned that there are many things that need to be taken into consideration when creating a recipe for two. For starters, ingredients need to be adjusted so you don't have a bunch of this 'n' that leftover, that ya don't really know what to do with. Plus, you've got to consider using smaller pan sizes and changes in cooking time.

If you're one of the over 50-million two-person households in the U.S., then you've got the right book in your hands. This book is great whether you're just starting out and learning how to cook for you and a significant other (or a very grateful roommate!) or you're newlyweds who love cooking together, but don't necessarily want to have so much food that your in-laws feel it's okay to stop by for dinner anytime they'd like. (If ya do want to invite 'em over, we've got other books for that!) Young families and empty nesters will appreciate it too, since we find that moms and dads sometimes end up cooking separate meals for themselves and their picky eaters, or that they forget how to cook just for two when those picky eaters grow up and move out! And let's not forget those young-at-heart seniors who grew up with homemade goodness and still want it, but don't want to eat leftovers for days or invest a lot of time or money in cooking, like they used to.

There are more than 130 quick and easy recipes in this book, all perfectly created for two. Each recipe features just a few simple steps and easy-to-find ingredients that you'll be able to pick up at any supermarket. Plus, with a full-page color photo for each recipe, you'll never be left wondering what the final dish should look like. We think you're going to like the helpful Test Kitchen hints and tips sprinkled throughout the book, too. It's just our way of ensuring that every recipe you make turns out picture-perfect.

Whether you're looking for recipes to make it easy for the two of you to rise 'n' shine in the mornings or fill-ya-up meals that'll put smiles on your faces after a long day, you'll find them here. And for those of you with a sweet tooth who avoid making dessert 'cause you're afraid you'll end up eating it all (we understand!), you're going to want to make sure you check out the decadent desserts designed for two.

So, what do you say we get going and start discovering some new favorites? After all, there's nothing better than sharing a meal with someone special and saying together...

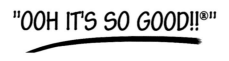

"OOH IT'S SO GOOD!!®"

Acknowledgements

Who would think that it would take so many people to create a cookbook for two? We sure wouldn't have if we hadn't worked on it ourselves. But the reality is that it does, and we are so thankful that we've assembled such a talented team over the years.

Patty Rosenthal
Test Kitchen Director

Howard Rosenthal
Chief Food Officer

Kelly Rusin
Photographer & Stylist

Merly Mesa
Editor

Jodi Flayman
Director of Publishing

Carol Ginsburg
Editor

Amy Magro
Dir. of Business Affairs

Jaime Gross
Business Assistant

Yolanda Reid
Brand Ambassador

Steve Ginsburg
Chief Executive Officer

Dave DiCarlo
Test Kitchen Assistant

Ana Cook
Website Editor

Roxana DeLima
Comptroller

Hal Silverman
Post Production
Hal Silverman Studio

Lorraine Dan
Book Design
Grand Design

Table of Contents

Tips to Help You $ave Money & Time at the Grocery Store

To make the most out of cooking for two, we've assembled some of our best Test Kitchen tips for saving you time and money. Keep these tips in mind the next time you go shopping for groceries, and you might just surprise yourself – they're really that helpful!

Meat Department:

- Make friends with the butcher. That way, they'll be more helpful in getting you the exact cut and size of meat you need, which will help reduce waste.

- If your supermarket only sells prepackaged meats or if you like to buy in bulk (which can usually save you up to 25%), be sure to properly repackage what you're not using in the next day or two. Be sure you label and date the bags, too!

Seafood Department:

- It's a good idea to buy shrimp Individually Quick Frozen (IQF), which just means that each individual piece of shrimp has been frozen separately from the others. The great thing about IQF is that you can easily take out what you need without having to thaw a whole "block." We've also found that the price of shrimp packed in large bags is usually less expensive per pound.

- Most supermarkets sell both fresh and frozen seafood. Fresh is nice if you plan on making it within a few days, but if that's not possible, we suggest picking up individually frozen fish fillets.

Produce Department:

- 6-ounce bags of greens, such as spinach, cut romaine, and mixed lettuces are perfect for two.

- Buy smaller-sized produce. Opt for smaller onions, instead of the big ones, or smaller-sized hearts of celery, instead of the large bunch.

- Buy precut fruits and vegetables. It might cost a little more per pound, but if you get just the amount you need you'll have less waste and spend less time prepping.

- Get acquainted with your supermarket's salad bar. Not only can you buy just the amount you need for your recipe, but oftentimes it's already cut the way you want it, so you can save time.

Dairy Aisle:

- Smaller-sized servings of dairy are easily found and are great for recipes made just for two:
    * Pints of milk
    * 6- and 8-ounce containers of yogurt
    * Single-serving containers of cottage cheese
- If you only need a small amount of cheese, check out the snack-sized packages.

Freezer Aisle:

- Stock up on frozen items, like vegetables, fruit, meat, chicken, and fish. Because they're perfectly preserved using a flash-freezing process, there's no rush to use them before they spoil.

- Look for frozen items that allow you to take out just what you need without having to thaw the whole package.

- Get a jump-start on baking by using frozen puff pastry and phyllo dough, which are especially perfect when you're creating recipes just for two.

Dry Goods Aisle:

- Smaller-sized packages are often just what you need when you're cooking for two:
    * 7- and 8-ounce cans of vegetables, sauces, and beans
    * Small cans and pouches of tuna, salmon, and crab
    * Small drink boxes of 100% juice for sauces and salad dressings

- Snack-sized packages are the perfect size and can usually be found right in the checkout aisle:
    * Chips for toppings
    * Cookies for pie crusts
    * Nuts for baking

From the Liquor Store:

- Rather than buying a big bottle of wine for a recipe that only needs a splash, you can buy individual-sized bottles. You may also want to consider using boxed wine, which has an airtight inner bag that prevents exposure to oxygen even after it's been opened. Boxed wine can last for weeks!

- Most liquor can be purchased in travel-sized bottles at all liquor stores. These smaller bottles are great when you only need a little liquor for a recipe.

- If the recipe calls for just a small amount of beer, you can often buy individual bottles instead of a whole 6-pack, that's if you're not a beer drinker, of course.

Packaged Foods:

- As with many packaged and canned foods, sizes may vary from brand to brand. Generally, the sizes indicated in the recipes are average sizes, but if you can't find the exact indicated package size, whatever is closest will usually do the trick.

- Buy broth or stock in smaller cans or packages, too. If you only need a small amount from a can, you can always freeze the rest in ice cube trays. Once your broth has frozen, be sure to repack them in resealable freezer bags for easy thawing.

- Don't forget to check out your store's bulk foods department for items like rice, grains, and dry beans, which will allow you to get the exact amount you need.

Serves/Makes/Portion Sizes:

- This is a "cooking for two" cookbook, so it would only make sense for all of the recipes in this book to have two servings, right? Of course it does! While that is the case for most of the recipes, you might find a few exceptions. For example, in some recipes you may see "Makes 6 cookies" because we felt there was no sense in making just 2 cookies (unless they're jumbo-sized!). Instead, we created the recipes to satisfy the appetites of two people.

30 Minutes or Less:

- We know how precious your time is, which is why so many of the recipes in this book are ready in just 30 minutes or less. Rather than expecting you to read each recipe to figure out which are the fastest, we've clearly marked those with "30 Minutes or Less" on the bottom of the recipes. Oh, and when we say 30 minutes or less, we're talking prep time and cook time. Isn't that great?

A Few Must-Have Basics:

- Since you plan on doing a lot of cooking for two, we think it's a great idea to pick up a few smaller-sized casserole dishes to round out your bakeware collection. We found that you can find some great buys at some of the big-box retailers or discount stores that carry kitchen items. We recommend purchasing a couple of 1- and 2-cup ramekins, a 1-quart baking dish, and a few shallow, individual oval baking dishes (like they use in restaurants for individual portions). You can probably get all of this for under $20!

Welcome to the Mr. Food Test Kitchen Family!

Whether you've been a fan of the Mr. Food Test Kitchen for years or were just recently introduced to us, we want to welcome you into our kitchen...and our family. Even though we've grown in many ways over the years, the one thing that hasn't changed is our philosophy for quick & easy cooking.

Over thirty years ago we began by sharing our recipes with you through the television screen. Today, not only is the Mr. Food Test Kitchen TV segment syndicated all over the country, but we've also proudly published over 50 best-selling cookbooks. That's not to mention the hugely popular MrFood.com and EverydayDiabeticRecipes.com. And for those of you who love to get social, we do too! You can find us online on Facebook, Twitter, Pinterest, and Instagram – boy, do we love connecting with you!

If you've got a passion for cooking (like we do!), then you know that the only thing better than curling up with a cookbook and drooling over the pictures is actually getting to taste the food. That's why we give you simple step-by-step instructions that make it feel like we're in your kitchen guiding you along the way. Your taste buds will be celebrating in no time!

By the way, now that you're part of the family, we want to let you in on a little secret...later this year we'll be launching all sorts of tools and bakeware to make your life in the kitchen even easier. Be sure to let your friends and family know, 'cause once everyone gets word of it, we're not sure how long they'll stay on the shelves!

So, whether you're new to the family or you've been a part of it from the very beginning, we want to thank you. You can bet there's always room at our table for you, because there's nothing better than sharing in all of the... "OOH IT'S SO GOOD!!®"

Patty   Howard   Kelly

Dedication:

It is with great honor that we dedicate this book to Art and Ethel Ginsburg, the founders of the Mr. Food brand. Their love of cooking for one another was a true inspiration as we created this book.

Eye-Opening Breakfasts

Fiesta Scramble in a Mug

This recipe is perfect for those busy weekday mornings because you can make it in no time. You can even get it ready the night before and cook it off at breakfast the next day. All you have to do after waking up and putting on the coffee is pop it into the microwave. Now the two of you can enjoy a hot and hearty breakfast anytime!

Makes 2

Ingredients

4 eggs

¼ cup milk

¼ cup frozen corn, thawed

2 tablespoons chopped red bell pepper

1 teaspoon chopped fresh cilantro

¼ teaspoon ground cumin

½ teaspoon hot sauce

2 tablespoons salsa

Preparation

1 Coat two microwave-safe coffee mugs with cooking spray.

2 In a medium bowl, whisk eggs and milk. Add remaining ingredients except salsa; mix well. Divide mixture equally into mugs. Microwave one mug 45 seconds; stir. Continue to microwave an additional 45 to 60 seconds, or until eggs are set. Repeat with remaining mug. [See Tip.]

3 Top both mugs with salsa and serve.

Test Kitchen Tip: *We don't recommend cooking both of these in the microwave at the same time. It will actually take longer and the eggs won't be as light and fluffy.*

Fancy Schmancy Eggs Benedict

How come the price of eggs Benedict is usually double what bacon, eggs and toast cost at almost every restaurant? We guess calling this combo some fancy schmancy name and topping it with Hollandaise sauce allows 'em to charge a crazy price. Rather than going out for this special breakfast, why not make it at home for two, for about what the tip would be?

Serves 2

Ingredients

1 (.9-ounce) package Hollandaise sauce mix

1 teaspoon lemon juice

1 tablespoon butter

4 slices Canadian bacon

4 cups water

¼ cup white vinegar

4 eggs

2 English muffins

1 tomato, sliced

Preparation

1 In a small saucepan, prepare Hollandaise sauce according to package directions; add lemon juice and keep warm over low heat, stirring occasionally.

2 In a medium skillet over low heat, melt butter; cook Canadian bacon 2 minutes per side, or until hot and edges are crispy.

3 In a large skillet, bring water and vinegar to a boil. Crack eggs one at a time and gently drop each into boiling mixture. Cook 4 to 6 minutes, or until the egg whites are set and the yolks are cooked to desired doneness.

4 Meanwhile, toast English muffins. Place on a plate and top each half with a slice of tomato and Canadian bacon. Using a slotted spoon, remove eggs from water and place one over each slice of bacon. Top with Hollandaise sauce and serve immediately.

Farm-Style Veggie-Stuffed Omelet

You're gonna want to bring both of your appetites to the breakfast table, 'cause this oversized and over-stuffed omelet is so big it's perfect for sharin'. And the best part, besides the taste, is that both of you can enjoy breakfast at the same time rather than one of you eating while the other one waits for their omelet to finish cooking. Now that's what we call a recipe for a good morning!

Serves 2

Ingredients

2 teaspoons vegetable oil

¼ cup diced
green bell pepper

2 tablespoons diced onion

¼ cup cherry tomatoes,
cut in half

¼ cup sliced fresh mushrooms

½ teaspoon garlic powder

¼ teaspoon salt

4 eggs

2 tablespoons
room temperature water

½ cup shredded cheddar cheese

Preparation

1 In an 8- to 10-inch non-stick skillet over medium heat, heat oil until hot. Add bell pepper, onion, tomatoes, mushrooms, garlic powder, and salt. Sauté 4 to 5 minutes, or until veggies are tender. Remove vegetables from skillet and set aside.

2 Coat the skillet with cooking spray and place over medium heat. In a bowl, beat eggs with water. Add to skillet, and with a rubber spatula, gently stir, pushing the cooked portion of the eggs to the center of the pan.

3 When the eggs firm up and are no longer liquidy, sprinkle half the omelet with the cheese and top with the veggie mixture. Cook until cheese is melted. To serve, slide the omelet out of the pan onto a platter, folding in half over the filling. Cut in half and enjoy.

Did You Know? *The key to making a light and fluffy omelet is to add a splash of water to the beaten eggs. The water should be at room temperature. If it's too hot it could cook the eggs, and if it's too cold it'll coagulate the proteins in the egg and make 'em rubbery when cooked. Whaddya think of that?*

30 MINUTES OR LESS

Avocado Egg Cups

We all know avocado makes a great topping for salads and is key to making guacamole, but in the Test Kitchen we knew we could do so much more with it. So, after lots of experimenting, we came up with this change-of-pace breakfast that'll have you falling in love with avocados in a whole new way.

Makes 2

Ingredients

1 avocado, cut in half and pitted (see Tip)

1 plum tomato, seeded and diced

2 tablespoons diced red onion

1 tablespoon chopped fresh cilantro

1 teaspoon finely diced jalapeño (optional)

2 teaspoons lime juice

½ teaspoon salt, divided

¼ teaspoon black pepper, divided

4 eggs

Preparation

1 Using a spoon, scoop the avocado out of the skin, keeping the shell intact. Dice avocado and place in a large bowl. Toss with tomato, onion, cilantro, jalapeño, if desired, lime juice, ¼ teaspoon salt, and ⅛ teaspoon pepper. Cover and refrigerate until ready to use.

2 In a medium bowl, beat eggs with remaining salt and pepper. Coat a non-stick skillet with cooking spray and heat over medium-high heat. Add eggs to skillet and scramble until set, stirring occasionally.

3 Evenly divide scrambled eggs into avocado shells and top with avocado mixture. Serve immediately.

Test Kitchen Tip: *Cutting an avocado is as easy as 1-2-3:*

1. Run a knife around the avocado lengthwise, cutting the skin and pulp in half.

2. Twist the two halves in opposite directions to separate.

3. Carefully insert a knife into the pit and twist to remove!

30 MINUTES OR LESS

Rancher's Breakfast Sandwiches

Decisions, decisions! The big question isn't whether you'll be making this for breakfast or for "brinner" (that's breakfast for dinner!), but how you're gonna eat this meal. Will you pick it up like a sandwich, or are you going to go all dainty and use a fork and knife? We started out eating it like a sandwich, but ended up using our utensils to pick up all the bits 'n' pieces left on the plate. It's that good!

Makes 2

Ingredients

4 slices frozen Texas toast

4 slices cheddar cheese

4 slices bacon

1 tablespoon butter

2 eggs

Hot sauce (optional)

Preparation

1 Prepare Texas toast according to package directions. Top each slice of toast with a slice of cheese and set aside.

2 Meanwhile, in a large skillet over medium heat, cook bacon 6 to 8 minutes, or until crispy; place bacon on a paper towel-lined plate, leaving the bacon drippings in the pan. Add butter to pan, and melt. Over medium heat, fry eggs to desired doneness.

3 Top each of 2 slices of toast with bacon, a fried egg, a splash of hot sauce, if desired, and remaining toast. Serve immediately.

Did You Know? *Hot peppers are considered an aphrodisiac, 'cause they're full of capsaicin, which is an ingredient that's said to have strong powers when it comes to the language of love. So, if you're looking to add a bit of romance to breakfast (or dinner), then keep that in mind. Hmm...is that what it means to "spice things up"?*

30 MINUTES OR LESS

Greek Breakfast Roll-Ups

Cozy up to breakfast alongside that special someone with this Mediterranean-inspired roll-up. It's just as good when you're kicking back and relaxing on the weekend, as it is when you're hurrying to get out the door on a weekday. And even though this recipe has Greek roots, we don't suggest you smash the plates like they often do at Greek weddings and restaurants. Wash 'em instead... it's a lot safer and way more practical!

Makes 2

Ingredients

4 eggs

1 tablespoon water

⅛ teaspoon salt

⅛ teaspoon black pepper

2 teaspoons butter

¼ cup chopped roasted red pepper, drained well

2 tablespoons sliced black olives, drained

¼ cup crumbled feta cheese

¼ teaspoon dried oregano

1 cup spinach leaves

2 (8-inch) spinach tortillas

Preparation

1 In a medium bowl, whisk eggs, water, salt, and pepper.

2 In a medium skillet over medium heat, melt butter; add egg mixture and scramble until almost set. Add roasted red pepper, olives, feta cheese, oregano, and spinach; stir gently until combined.

3 Remove from heat and evenly divide egg mixture onto the middle of each tortilla. Fold the edge of the tortilla that's closest to you over the filling, then fold in each side and roll tightly, ending with the seam side down.

4 Cut in half and serve immediately.

So Many Options: *Although we made these with spinach tortillas, if you'd rather, feel free to swap 'em out with sun-dried tomato, whole wheat, or even plain ones.*

30 MINUTES OR LESS

Ham & Swiss Omelet Rounds

We understand that you've got places to go and people to see, which is exactly why we came up with this recipe for omelet rounds. They can be enjoyed fresh out of the oven, or made ahead of time and frozen until you're ready to eat 'em! And if you're the first one out the door in the morning, ya might want to leave a note on the kitchen counter to remind your significant other that there's breakfast waiting for them, too!

Serves 2

Ingredients

3 eggs

¼ cup chopped cooked ham

⅓ cup shredded Swiss cheese

2 tablespoons sliced scallions

⅛ teaspoon salt

⅛ teaspoon black pepper

Preparation

1 Preheat oven to 350 degrees F. Coat 4 muffin cups with cooking spray. (Yup, most muffin tins have 6 or 12 cups but here we're only using 4 of them. It's perfectly fine to leave the rest empty.)

2 In a medium bowl, combine all ingredients; mix well, then spoon into muffin cups.

3 Bake 20 to 25 minutes, or until eggs are set. Cool for a minute before running a knife around the edges of each cup. Remove from muffin cups and serve immediately.

Mix 'n' Match: *Feel free to experiment with different cheeses. You may want to try Swiss one time and Gouda another time. There are no rules when it comes to using what you like best!*

30 MINUTES OR LESS

All-in-One Breakfast Casserole

Here in the Test Kitchen, we're big fans of comforting casseroles. And like many of you, when we think casseroles, we never think of making 'em for breakfast. But one day we were challenged by a viewer to create a mouthwatering casserole that combined all of their favorite breakfast ingredients, and this recipe was born. So, let us introduce you to the ultimate breakfast casserole that's weekday-easy and will change the way you think about breakfast forever.

Serves 2

Ingredients

2 frozen hash brown patties

4 cooked breakfast sausage links, cut into ½-inch pieces

½ cup shredded sharp cheddar cheese

3 eggs

2 tablespoons milk

½ teaspoon dry mustard

¼ teaspoon salt

⅛ teaspoon black pepper

Preparation

1 Preheat oven to 400 degrees F. Coat a 2-cup baking dish or an 8- x 4-inch loaf pan with cooking spray.

2 Coat a small skillet with cooking spray, and over medium-high heat, cook the hash brown patties on both sides, until golden. Place hash brown patties in baking dish and top with sausage and cheese.

3 In a small bowl, whisk remaining ingredients; pour over cheese. (If you're using a loaf pan, this will only fill it up about ¼ of the way, no worries!) Cover and bake 20 minutes. Uncover and bake an additional 5 to 10 minutes, or until set. Let stand 5 minutes before serving.

Blueberry Cheesecake French Toast

You won't have to travel farther than your own pantry or fridge to find the ingredients for this decadent breakfast. Crispy cereal gives this French toast a nice crunch, while the cinnamon-cream cheese mixture makes it ooey-gooey delicious. You want to see how fast you can get your significant other to the kitchen? Start heatin' up the skillet!

Serves 2

Ingredients

2 eggs

2 tablespoons milk

1 teaspoon vanilla extract

2 cups cornflake cereal, coarsely crushed

2 tablespoons sugar

½ teaspoon ground cinnamon

¼ cup cream cheese, softened

2 tablespoons confectioners' sugar

2 tablespoons blueberry preserves

4 slices country white bread

2 tablespoons butter

Preparation

1 In a shallow bowl, whisk eggs, milk, and vanilla until well combined; set aside. In another shallow bowl, combine cereal, sugar, and cinnamon; mix well and set aside.

2 In a small bowl, combine cream cheese and confectioners' sugar; mix well, then stir in preserves. Spread equally over 2 slices of bread. Top with remaining bread slices, forming sandwiches.

3 In a large skillet or griddle over medium heat, melt butter. Dip each sandwich into egg mixture, then into cereal mixture, completely coating both sides. Cook sandwiches 2 to 4 minutes per side, or until golden. Slice in half diagonally, and serve.

So Many Options: *If you're not a blueberry lover, feel free to swap out the flavor of preserves for whatever you prefer. You can even swap out the preserves with jam. However, we suggest that you don't use jelly as it makes the filling loose. As for the topping, you can serve these as-is, sprinkle on some confectioners' sugar, or drizzle on the syrup.*

30 MINUTES OR LESS

Banana Split Pancakes

If your travels ever take you to Ft. Lauderdale, Florida, then you have to stop by Jaxson's Ice Cream Parlor. It's been voted one of the best old-fashioned ice cream parlors in the country. It also happens to be one of our favorite places to, shall we say, "pig out!" After ordering one of their over-the-top banana split sundaes, we got inspired to create these over-the-top breakfast pancakes that'll leave you wishing you had a dessert-style breakfast more often!

Serves 2

Ingredients

1 cup pancake mix

¼ cup milk

½ cup melted vanilla ice cream

1 egg

2 tablespoons mini semisweet chocolate chips

2 tablespoons butter, divided

1 banana, sliced in half lengthwise and then widthwise

Whipped topping for garnish

Chocolate-flavored syrup for garnish

2 maraschino cherries

1 tablespoon chopped walnuts

Preparation

1 In a large bowl, combine pancake mix, milk, ice cream, (Yes, ice cream, and make sure it's melted!) and egg. Mix until thoroughly combined. Stir in chocolate chips.

2 On a nonstick griddle or skillet over medium heat, melt 1 tablespoon butter. Pour ¼ cup of batter per pancake onto griddle, making sure the batter is mixed well before scooping, so the chips don't sink to the bottom of the bowl. Cook 1 minute, or until bubbles start to form on top of pancakes. Flip pancakes, and cook until golden. Repeat with remaining batter, adding more butter as needed. Cover to keep warm.

3 Now for the fun part: place 2 pancakes on each plate and top with 2 pieces of banana. Dollop each with whipped cream, drizzle with chocolate syrup, and top with a cherry and walnuts.

Test Kitchen Tip: *We discovered that adding the melted ice cream to the batter makes these extra rich. Plus, since the ice cream is brimming with cream, vanilla and sugar, it's like adding three ingredients in one, which is handy when you're only cooking for two.*

30 MINUTES OR LESS

Apple Bacon Maple Oatmeal

They say an apple a day keeps the doctor away, and that's what we were going for when we came up with this great nutritious breakfast that's loaded with more than 8 grams of fiber. We've also heard it said that cinnamon is a good source of antioxidants that can help prevent heart disease and diabetes, too. Don't you just love when something so tasty is packed with all sorts of good stuff?

Serves 2

Ingredients

2-¼ cups water

1-½ cups quick-cooking oatmeal

½ teaspoon ground cinnamon

⅛ teaspoon salt

½ apple, peeled and diced

2 tablespoons maple syrup

2 tablespoons crumbled crisply cooked bacon

Preparation

1 In a saucepan over medium heat, bring water to a boil. Add oatmeal, cinnamon, salt, and apples, and cook 1-½ minutes, stirring occasionally.

2 Remove from heat and stir in syrup and bacon. Spoon into bowls and serve immediately.

Note: If ya want, feel free to top this off with some extra cut-up apples, more bacon, and a pat of butter. It'll make it even more incredible.

Good For You! Studies show that oatmeal may lower blood pressure, improve cholesterol, and aid in the fight against heart disease. It's no wonder why oatmeal is considered a breakfast superfood. Plus, it tastes pretty darn good, too!

30 MINUTES OR LESS

Cinnamon Bun for Two

If you're the type of person who can walk past one of those cinnamon bun places at the mall and not even slow down to take in all the goodness, then you might as well just turn the page. On the other hand, if you purposely walk out of your way to see if there are any cinnamon buns coming out fresh from the oven, then roll up your sleeves and start cookin'.

Serves 2

Ingredients

¼ cup applesauce

2 tablespoons vegetable oil

2 tablespoons milk

½ teaspoon vanilla extract

⅔ cup all-purpose flour

6 tablespoons packed light brown sugar

2-½ teaspoons ground cinnamon, divided

½ teaspoon baking powder

⅛ teaspoon salt

1 tablespoon chopped pecans

CREAM CHEESE ICING
2 tablespoons cream cheese, softened

5 tablespoons confectioners' sugar

2 teaspoons milk

Preparation

1 Coat a microwave-safe cereal bowl (about 2 cups) with cooking spray.

2 In a small bowl, combine applesauce, oil, milk, vanilla, flour, light brown sugar, ¼ teaspoon cinnamon, the baking powder, and salt. Reserve 1 tablespoon batter in another small bowl and place remaining batter in the cereal bowl.

3 Add remaining 2-¼ teaspoons cinnamon to 1 tablespoon batter that you set aside, then swirl mixture into batter in bowl.

4 Microwave 2 minutes, or until center is set. Let cool 4 to 5 minutes, then invert onto a plate.

5 In a small bowl, combine Icing ingredients, stirring until smooth. Spread on cinnamon bun, sprinkle with nuts, and serve immediately.

Test Kitchen Tip: This tastes way better when served warm, and when shared!

Banana Bread Muffins

We took our best banana bread recipe and scaled it down to make four incredibly moist banana bread muffins, so you can both enjoy two muffins each. Sure, it may sound like a lot, but rest assured, once you get a taste of these, you're going to want a second one to devour. And the great thing is, that they're just as good right out of the oven as they are slathered with butter.

Makes 4 muffins

Ingredients

1 ripe banana, mashed

2 tablespoons vegetable oil

1 egg

½ teaspoon vanilla extract

½ cup biscuit baking mix

¼ cup sugar

3 tablespoons chopped walnuts, divided

1 tablespoon brown sugar

1 teaspoon all-purpose flour

Preparation

1 Preheat oven to 350 degrees F. Line 4 cups of a muffin tin with paper liners.

2 In a medium bowl, combine banana, oil, egg, vanilla, baking mix, sugar, and 2 tablespoons walnuts. Stir with a wooden spoon until thoroughly mixed. Spoon evenly into paper liners.

3 In a small bowl, combine brown sugar, flour, and remaining tablespoon of walnuts; sprinkle over muffins.

4 Bake 15 to 18 minutes, or until a toothpick inserted in center comes out clean. Remove to a wire rack to cool.

Test Kitchen Tip: *If your bananas aren't very ripe place them, unpeeled, on a tray in your toaster oven, preheated to 300 degrees F, for 30 to 40 minutes. Carefully peel them, let them cool, and you're good to go.*

30 MINUTES OR LESS

Tropical Pineapple Spinach Smoothie

If you have a hard time getting up in the morning, then make this smoothie for a great way to start your day. After all, it's packed with all sorts of nutrients our bodies need, and when it comes to taste, it's simply yummy-delicious.

Serves 2

Ingredients

1 cup frozen pineapple chunks

1 cup fresh spinach

1 banana, peeled

¾ cup almond milk

½ cup pineapple juice

Preparation

1 In a blender, combine all ingredients and blend until smooth. Pour into glasses and serve immediately.

Note: If you're using fresh pineapple, don't forget to add a cup of ice, to make it extra slushy.

Berry-licious Smoothie

Start your day the easy way with a smoothie you can enjoy while on the go. It sure is a lot easier to drink a smoothie than trying to balance a bowl of mixed berries, a cup of Greek yogurt, and a big glass of milk, all while walking out the door!

Serves 2

Ingredients

2 cups frozen mixed berries

¾ cup milk

½ cup vanilla Greek yogurt

1-½ teaspoons vanilla extract

3 tablespoons sugar

Preparation

1 In a blender, combine all ingredients and blend until smooth. Pour into glasses and serve immediately.

Simple Salads
& Sandwiches

Apple Orchard Kale with Shaved Cheddar

A tasty trend among salad lovers is to swap out lettuce for kale. That's because kale is packed with all sorts of vitamins and minerals, making it what's known as a "superfood." Besides that, kale has a pretty long shelf life, which means you don't have to worry about your salad going to waste from one day to the next. With it being so tasty, nutritious, and long-lasting, you really can't miss!

Serves 2

Ingredients

4 cups chopped kale

1 apple, cored and cubed

¼ cup chopped celery

2 tablespoons dried cranberries

2 teaspoons sunflower seeds

Block of white cheddar cheese

DRESSING

¼ cup olive oil

2 tablespoons honey

1 tablespoon apple cider vinegar

1 tablespoon Dijon mustard

⅛ teaspoon salt

Preparation

1 Place kale in a medium bowl. Top with apple, celery, cranberries, and sunflower seeds.

2 In a small bowl, whisk dressing ingredients. Drizzle over salad; toss gently to coat.

3 With a vegetable peeler, shave the cheese (almost like you're peeling carrots) over the top of the salad.

Decisions, Decisions: *If you don't have apple cider vinegar in your pantry, you can always use another type of vinegar, like red wine, rice, or white balsamic.*

Southern Stacked Cornbread Salad

If you've ever been to a real Southern picnic or potluck dinner, then we bet you've had a version of this recipe. Of course, the ones you've probably seen are usually big enough to serve a small village. With our scaled-down version that's perfect for two, you can now enjoy the best dish at the potluck buffet, without having to make enough for an army.

Serves 2

Ingredients

2 corn muffins, crumbled and divided

½ (16-ounce) can pinto beans, rinsed and drained

½ green bell pepper, chopped

½ cup ranch dressing, divided

½ cup frozen corn, thawed

1 tomato, chopped

4 slices bacon, cooked and crumbled

½ cup shredded Monterey Jack cheese

1 scallion, sliced

Preparation

1 In a medium glass bowl, place half the crumbled corn muffins, the beans, the bell pepper, ¼ cup of the dressing, the corn, tomato, bacon, remaining corn muffins, the cheese, and scallion.

2 Right before serving, drizzle remaining dressing over the salad and dig in.

Test Kitchen Tip: *Rather than cooking and crumbling bacon, feel free to buy pre-crumbled cooked bacon. Or if ya want to lighten things up, you can always use turkey bacon and reduced-fat ranch dressing.*

30 MINUTES OR LESS

Tuscan Bread Salad

What we love about this bread salad is that it's actually better if ya make it with leftover bread that's starting to go stale. And if there're only two of you at home, there's a pretty good chance of that happening. So, rather than tossing out that day-old bread, now you can turn it into the best salad ever. Yup, the drier the texture of the bread, but not to the point that it's rock hard, the better the salad...really!

Serves 2

Ingredients

3 slices thick-cut Italian bread, cut into 1-inch cubes

Cooking spray

1 tomato, cut into 1-inch chunks

½ cucumber, seeded and cubed

¼ cup thinly sliced red onion

⅓ cup Italian dressing

½ teaspoon Italian seasoning

⅛ teaspoon black pepper

Preparation

1 Preheat oven to 300 degrees F. Place bread cubes on a baking sheet and spray with cooking spray. Bake bread cubes 6 to 8 minutes, or until golden. At this point they should be nice and crispy. Remove from oven and cool.

2 Meanwhile, in a large bowl, combine tomato, cucumber, onion, dressing, Italian seasoning, and pepper; mix well. Let marinate 15 minutes.

3 Add bread cubes to the veggies and toss to coat. Serve immediately.

Test Kitchen Tip: *When it comes to the Italian dressing, feel free to use whatever's most convenient for you: bottled, homemade, or semi-homemade, which starts off with a package of dry seasoning mix.*

Fresh Citrus Beet Salad

This vibrant-colored salad will make you feel like you're eating right off of a fancy café menu. And it's not just the colors that make this such a "bright" salad, it's the citrusy taste, too. Every ingredient, from the crunchy nuts to the creamy goat cheese, gives it an extra-special taste. Remember, just because you're only cooking for two doesn't mean you can't get a little fancy every now and then. So, bon appétit!

Serves 2

Ingredients

¼ cup store-bought Italian dressing

2 tablespoons sugar

½ teaspoon poppy seeds

¼ cup chopped walnuts

2 tablespoons maple syrup

4 cups mixed baby salad greens

1 (8.25-ounce) can sliced beets, drained and cut in half

1 orange, peeled and cut into sections

2 tablespoons crumbled goat cheese

Preparation

1 In a small bowl, whisk together Italian dressing, sugar, and poppy seeds until the sugar is dissolved; set aside.

2 In a small skillet over medium heat, toast walnuts 3 to 4 minutes, or until they start to brown, stirring occasionally. Add syrup and stir until evenly coated; let cool.

3 Place greens in a shallow bowl. Top with beets, orange sections, walnuts, and cheese. Drizzle with dressing and serve.

Did You Know? You can often find freshly cooked whole beets shrink-wrapped in plastic, which ensures a longer shelf life, right in the produce section of your market. They are super convenient and mighty tasty. So look for them the next time you're there!

30 MINUTES OR LESS

The Simplest Greek Salad Ever

The Greeks love their olives (doesn't everybody?). In fact, as far back as ancient times, olives were used in everything from skin and hair care to crowning Olympic winners. So, it's no wonder that the traditional Greek salad we know and love today features Greek-grown Kalamata olives (those are the purplish-black ones). All you need is a couple of forks and an appetite to enjoy this salad!

Serves 2

Ingredients

½ cucumber, cut into ½-inch chunks

1 tomato, cut into 1-inch chunks

½ red onion, cut into ½-inch chunks

¼ cup Kalamata olives

¼ cup olive oil

2 tablespoons red wine vinegar

1 teaspoon lemon juice

½ teaspoon dried oregano

½ teaspoon garlic powder

½ teaspoon salt

2 cups chopped romaine lettuce

¼ cup cubed feta cheese

Preparation

1 In a medium bowl, combine cucumber, tomato, onion, and olives.

2 In a small bowl, whisk oil, vinegar, lemon juice, oregano, garlic powder, and salt. Pour over vegetables and toss until coated. (You can serve this now as instructed below or you may want to chill this a few hours first, that's up to you.)

3 Place romaine on a platter. Spoon vegetable mixture over lettuce, top with cheese, and serve.

Did You Know? You can often save money and time by buying small amounts of olives and cut up veggies from your supermarket's salad bar. They may cost a few more cents per pound, but you can buy just the amount you need, which is great when you are cooking for two.

30 MINUTES OR LESS

Balsamic-Glazed Bistro Salad

This recipe was inspired by the gourmet salads served at outdoor bistros around the world. Sure, it may look and taste fancy, but it's really simple to put together. What makes it so amazing is the way the tangy-yet-sweet balsamic reduction compliments the sharpness of the blue cheese and the smokiness of the bacon. When it's teamed up with some crusty bread and white wine, it'll feel like you've turned your kitchen into a bistro.

Serves 2

Ingredients

1 cup balsamic vinegar

½ cup light brown sugar

1 whole romaine heart, cut in half

6 cherry tomatoes, cut in half

2 slices red onion

2 tablespoons crumbled blue cheese

2 tablespoons crumbled crispy bacon

Preparation

1 In a medium saucepan over high heat, bring balsamic vinegar to a boil. Stir in brown sugar, reduce heat to low, and simmer 15 minutes, or until mixture thickens slightly. Remove from heat.

2 Meanwhile, place each romaine half on a plate. Top evenly with tomatoes, onion, blue cheese, and bacon. Drizzle with balsamic glaze and serve.

Note: If there's any leftover balsamic glaze, make sure ya store it in an airtight container in the fridge, until the next time you get the hankerin' for this salad. Then, all you have to do is pop it in the microwave for a few seconds to warm slightly, and you're good to go.

Test Kitchen Tip: *To make the romaine extra crisp and fresh-tasting, soak the whole head in ice cold water for about ten minutes, then drain it really well before cutting in half.*

10-Minute Shrimp Salad

Sometimes a simple salad topped off with a few shrimp is all we need for lunch or a light dinner, but shrimp can be a bit pricey if you buy just a few at the seafood counter. By buying 'em in bulk from the freezer section and thawing just what you need at a time, you can save a bundle! This just proves that if you plan ahead, the two of you can eat like kings without spending a king's ransom.

Serves 2

Ingredients

3 cups chopped romaine lettuce

¼ cup chopped celery

¼ cup chopped red bell pepper

1 hard-boiled egg, cut into quarters

6 large peeled and cooked shrimp, thawed if frozen

DRESSING

3 tablespoons mayonnaise

3 tablespoons cocktail sauce

1 teaspoon lemon juice

⅛ teaspoon salt

Pinch of cayenne pepper

1 teaspoon chopped fresh parsley (optional)

Preparation

1 Evenly divide lettuce onto 2 serving plates. Top each with celery, red bell pepper, egg, and shrimp.

2 In a small bowl, mix dressing ingredients. Spoon dressing over salad and serve.

Note: You can always turn up the heat on these by adding a bit more cayenne pepper to the dressing. Just keep in mind, a little goes a long way.

Waste-Not, Want-Not Marinated Cucumbers

Do you ever find that by the time you're just about to use up all the produce you bought earlier in the week it's starting to look pretty shabby? If you do, then you've gotta try this salad. Ya see, it calls for a whole cucumber and some onion, both of which have a pretty long shelf life, if stored properly. That means there's very little waste, especially when compared to what's in a traditional green salad.

Serves 2

Ingredients

1 large cucumber, thinly sliced

½ cup thinly sliced onion

¼ cup white vinegar

¼ cup water

1 teaspoon vegetable oil

2 tablespoons sugar

1 garlic clove, minced

½ teaspoon salt

⅛ teaspoon black pepper

1 tablespoon chopped fresh dill, or 1 teaspoon dried dillweed

Preparation

1 In a large bowl, combine cucumber and onion; set aside.

2 In a large saucepan, combine vinegar, water, oil, sugar, garlic, and salt; bring to a boil, stirring frequently. Pour mixture (yes, while it's still warm) over cucumber and onion; add pepper and dill and mix well.

3 Refrigerate 4 hours, or until chilled.

Note: When it comes to the skin of the cucumber, you can leave it on, peel part of it, or take it all off...that's up to you.

Did You Know? Cucumbers are best when stored in a cool, but not cold environment. That means they're best kept on your kitchen counter, out of direct sunlight, as long as your house is on the cool side.

Tango Chicken Salad with Avocado

Typically, if we were to make chicken salad for a crowd, it would make sense for us to boil up a bunch of chicken breasts or pull the meat off a few rotisserie chickens. But when cooking for only two, we found it's a lot easier, and often less expensive, if we use the cooked chicken that's in the freezer or refrigerated aisle of your supermarket. It doesn't get much easier than that!

Serves 2

Ingredients

¼ cup mayonnaise

2 teaspoons lime juice

¼ teaspoon salt

⅛ teaspoon black pepper

2 cups cooked chicken, cut into ½-inch cubes

1 tablespoon chopped red bell pepper

2 tablespoons chopped fresh cilantro

2 lettuce leaves

1 avocado, cut in half, pitted, and sliced

Preparation

1 In a medium bowl, combine mayonnaise, lime juice, salt, and pepper; mix well. Stir in chicken, bell pepper, and cilantro.

2 Spoon chicken mixture over lettuce leaves (as for the type of lettuce, you can use whatever kind you have on hand) and top with sliced avocado. Serve immediately.

Test Kitchen Tip: *Not exactly sure how to cut an avocado, check out page 8 (Avocado Egg Cups) for a few easy tips.*

Ooey-Gooey Bacon Grilled Cheese

This recipe should really come with a warning, because once you take a bite you'll have a hard time going back to your plain old grilled cheese again. No, really. This one is so creamy, gooey, and bacon-y delicious, it'll set the bar for all the other grilled cheese sandwiches that follow it. Look, you can pass this one by, but why would ya want to?

Serves 2

Ingredients

2 tablespoons mayonnaise

2 tablespoons cream cheese, softened

½ cup shredded cheddar cheese

½ cup shredded mozzarella cheese

¼ teaspoon garlic powder

¼ cup crumbled crispy bacon

4 slices sourdough bread

2 tablespoons butter, softened

Preparation

1 In a medium bowl mix mayonnaise and cream cheese until light and fluffy. Stir in cheddar cheese, mozzarella cheese, garlic powder, and bacon until well combined.

2 Spread 2 slices of bread evenly with cheese mixture. Top with remaining bread. Spread butter on both sides of sandwiches.

3 In a skillet over medium heat, cook until golden on both sides and cheese is melted.

So Many Options: Is there another bread you love or have on hand? Go ahead and use it! We've tried this with homestyle white bread, whole wheat, and even pumpernickel. Each one gave this combo its own special twist.

Wrapped-Up Baked Italian Heroes

Here is a great recipe for those nights when the two of you aren't eating at the same time. All you have to do is assemble these overstuffed subs and wrap 'em in foil. You can even do it the day before if ya want. Then, come dinnertime, pop one or both of these in your toaster oven just long enough to warm 'em through, until the cheese is all melty inside.

Serves 2

Ingredients

3 tablespoons prepared pesto

2 tablespoons mayonnaise

2 (6- to-8-inch) hoagie rolls, split

¼ pound sliced deli ham

¼ pound sliced deli salami

¼ cup roasted red pepper slices, drained well

4 slices mozzarella cheese

¼ cup banana pepper rings, drained

Preparation

1 Preheat oven to 375 degrees F. In a small bowl, mix pesto and mayonnaise and spread on cut sides of rolls.

2 Layer bottom halves of each roll with ham, salami, roasted red pepper, cheese, and banana pepper rings; place tops on rolls. Wrap each sandwich tightly in a piece of aluminum foil.

3 Bake 12 to 15 minutes, or until hot and the cheese is melted. Carefully remove aluminum foil, and serve.

Test Kitchen Tip: *This is one of those "there are no rules" recipes. So, feel free to toss in whatever you have on hand. Maybe some sliced black olives, pepperoncini, or giardiniera...you get the idea.*

30 MINUTES OR LESS

Pub-Style Roast Beef Sandwiches

If you're looking for a dinner that'll warm ya up and bring a smile to your face, without having to do a whole lot of work, this saucy roast beef sandwich is it. Full of comforting flavors, it's the kind of sandwich that you'll want to eat while watching reruns of your favorite classic shows. Isn't it great when the simple things make you feel all warm and fuzzy inside?

Serves 2

Ingredients

¾ cup all-purpose flour, divided

1-⅛ teaspoons salt, divided

½ teaspoon black pepper, divided

½ cup vegetable oil

1 onion, thinly sliced and separated into rings

1-½ cups beef broth

½ pound thinly sliced deli roast beef

4 slices white bread

Preparation

1 In a medium bowl, combine ½ cup flour, 1 teaspoon salt, and ¼ teaspoon pepper; mix well.

2 In a large skillet over medium-high heat, heat oil until hot. Place onion rings in flour, coating well, then carefully place in hot oil. Fry 6 to 8 minutes, or until golden, turning as needed. Drain on a paper towel-lined plate. (These will look more like onion straws than onion rings).

3 In the same skillet over medium heat, stir the remaining ¼ cup flour into the oil and cook about 1 minute, or until golden, scraping any bits of onion from the bottom of the pan. Add broth, and remaining ⅛ teaspoon salt and ¼ teaspoon pepper, and cook until thickened. (If you prefer your gravy a little thinner, add a bit more beef broth.) Add roast beef and cook 3 to 5 minutes, or until heated through.

4 Place 2 slices of bread on each plate, slightly overlapping, and spoon the hot roast beef and gravy over them. Top with fried onions and go to town.

Smothered Patty Melts

If you've ever wondered what the heck the difference between a patty melt and a cheeseburger is, you're not alone. The main difference is that a patty melt is served on rye bread that's been toasted on a griddle and loaded with onions, while a cheeseburger is....well, you know what it is! So, for this recipe, put away your buns, take out your griddle (or skillet), and start toasting!

Serves 2

Ingredients

2 tablespoons butter, divided

1 small onion, thinly sliced

¾ pound ground beef

¼ teaspoon salt

⅛ teaspoon black pepper

4 slices rye bread

4 slices Swiss cheese

¼ cup Thousand Island dressing

Preparation

1 On a griddle or in a large skillet over medium-high heat, melt 1 tablespoon butter; sauté onions 6 to 8 minutes, or until they start to brown. Remove to a bowl and cover.

2 Meanwhile, in a small bowl, combine ground beef, salt, and pepper. Shape into 2 oval patties.

3 On the same griddle over medium heat, cook patties 5 to 7 minutes per side, or until desired doneness. Remove from griddle and keep warm.

4 Spread remaining butter over one side of each slice of bread. Place on griddle buttered-side down, place a slice of cheese on top, and toast until golden and cheese begins to melt.

5 Now, to put it all together, place a slice of toasted bread (cheese side up) on each plate and top each with a patty, half the onions, and half the dressing. Top with the other slice of toasted bread (this time cheese side down). Now open up wide and enjoy!

30 MINUTES OR LESS

Very Sloppy Joes

Every time we serve this, there always seems to be a discussion as to whether we should eat it with a fork and knife or if it's ok to pick it up and eat it like the big messy sandwich that it is. Without taking sides, all we'll say is make sure ya have plenty of napkins on hand. Now, we'll let the two of you decide the best way to eat this without getting in the middle.

Serves 2

Ingredients

1 tablespoon vegetable oil

¾ pound lean ground turkey

½ cup chopped onion

½ teaspoon garlic powder

¼ teaspoon salt

¼ teaspoon black pepper

¾ cup ketchup

½ cup barbecue sauce

2 teaspoons Worcestershire sauce

2 hamburger buns, toasted

Preparation

1 In a large skillet over medium-high heat, heat oil until hot. Cook turkey, onion, garlic powder, salt, and pepper, stirring until turkey crumbles and is no longer pink.

2 Stir in ketchup, barbecue sauce, and Worcestershire sauce. Reduce heat to low and simmer 8 to 10 minutes, or until heated through, stirring occasionally. Serve on buns.

A Little Lighter: When it comes to ground turkey, we recommend using ground turkey breast rather than whole ground turkey as it's lower in fat and calories.

Savory Soups, Stews, & Chilis

Beef Barley Soup

Greek diners and Old World delis sure know how to serve up hearty helpings of this beefy soup. Our pint-sized version is so good, you may want to consider writing your local deli or diner a Dear John letter. Tell 'em you fell in love with your own homemade version and there's no going back!

Serves 2

Ingredients

1 tablespoon vegetable oil

½ pound beef stew meat, cut into ½-inch chunks

¼ cup chopped onion

1 cup sliced fresh mushrooms

1 carrot, coarsely diced

3 cups beef broth

¼ teaspoon salt

¼ teaspoon black pepper

⅓ cup quick-cooking pearl barley

Preparation

1 In a large saucepan over high heat, heat oil until hot. Add beef, onion, mushrooms, and carrot; sauté 6 to 8 minutes, or until they begin to brown.

2 Add broth, salt, and pepper; bring to a boil. Reduce heat to low, cover, and simmer 40 minutes, or until beef is tender, stirring occasionally.

3 Stir in barley and simmer an additional 15 to 20 minutes, or until barley is tender. Serve immediately.

Serving Suggestion: *Don't forget – make sure you have plenty of crusty rye or sourdough bread on hand for dunking!*

Cantina Tortilla Soup

We're taking you on a trip to your favorite Mexican cantina with this restaurant-inspired dish that's so bold and flavorful, it'll leave both of you saying, "Ole!" Want to add even more of an authentic cantina feel? How about grabbing your sombreros and maracas? (C'mon, we know you've got 'em!)

Serves 2

Ingredients

1 tablespoon vegetable oil

1 boneless, skinless chicken breast cut into ½-inch chunks

½ red bell pepper, coarsely chopped

1 clove garlic, minced

2 cups chicken broth

½ cup frozen corn

½ cup salsa

1 tablespoon chopped fresh cilantro

1 cup tortilla chips

Preparation

1 In a large saucepan over medium heat, heat oil until hot. Add chicken and bell pepper and cook about 5 minutes, or until chicken is browned, stirring frequently.

2 Stir in garlic, chicken broth, corn, and salsa; bring to a boil. Reduce heat to low and simmer 5 minutes, or until chicken is no longer pink.

3 Stir in cilantro, ladle into bowls, and serve with tortilla chips.

Test Kitchen Tip: *Before you toss out that almost empty bag of chips (the one that has only a few broken ones left in the bottom), think twice. Those crushed chips are perfect for breading chicken or using as a topping on soups and casseroles.*

30 MINUTES OR LESS

Pub-Style
Beer 'n' Cheese Soup

Before your guests drink up all your beer at the next tailgate or football party, set aside a can so you can make this pub-style cheese soup that's unbelievable. Ya see, the combo of sharp cheese with the malt of the beer is just perfect. And when you add in a dash or two of hot sauce you can really kick up the flavor!

Serves 2

Ingredients

1 cup milk

¾ cup beer, divided

1 cup processed cheese spread

¾ cup chicken broth

½ teaspoon Worcestershire sauce

2 dashes Sriracha sauce (hot sauce)

2 tablespoons cornstarch

Preparation

1 In a large saucepan over medium heat, combine milk and ½ cup beer. Cook until heated through, stirring constantly.

2 Add cheese spread, broth, Worcestershire sauce, and hot sauce. Reduce heat to low and cook until heated through, stirring constantly.

3 In a small bowl, combine cornstarch and remaining ¼ cup beer; stir in to cheese mixture. Simmer 5 minutes or until thickened, stirring constantly. (Do not boil.)

Fancy it Up: *After dishin this' up, why not drizzle the top of each bowl with a bit of Sriracha sauce. It'll kick up the flavor and add an extra dose of fun, too!*

Smoky Cheddar Corn Soup

You can always count on the smell of something rich and hearty wafting through country kitchens - it's part of what makes them so welcoming. Now, you can bring some of those warm, country kitchen feelings to your home by serving up big bowls of this cheesy corn soup, loaded with plenty of smoky bacon.

Serves 2

Ingredients

1 (10-½-ounce) can cream of chicken soup

1 cup chicken broth

1 cup frozen corn

1 cup chopped cooked chicken

1 cup shredded cheddar cheese

½ teaspoon onion powder

¼ teaspoon black pepper

1 tablespoon bacon bits

Preparation

1 In a large saucepan over medium-high heat, heat cream of chicken soup, broth, corn, and chicken, until it begins to boil, stirring occasionally.

2 Reduce heat to low and stir in remaining ingredients, making sure to add the cheese slowly, so it melts smoothly. Simmer about 10 minutes, or until heated through, stirring often.

Test Kitchen Tip: If you feel like you throw away more chicken broth than you actually have the chance to use, then we've got a suggestion: freeze it. Yep, you can freeze your chicken broth in water bottles, just don't overfill 'em. That way, when a recipe calls for chicken broth, you can just thaw the amount you need.

30 MINUTES OR LESS

Tomato Soup with Parmesan Dippers

Do you remember when Mom used to serve tomato soup from a can, with a side of grilled cheese for dipping? Well, how about tonight you put away the canned soup and make this homemade version of one of your favorite childhood meals instead? Our tomato soup is thick, rich, and extra creamy, making it perfect for dipping into. While ya dip and slurp, you two can swap stories about what other tasty foods you grew up with!

Serves 2

Ingredients

1 plain bagel

Cooking spray

1 tablespoon shredded Parmesan cheese

2 tablespoons butter

¼ cup chopped onion

1 tablespoon all-purpose flour

1-½ cups milk

¾ teaspoon salt

¼ teaspoon black pepper

1 teaspoon sugar

½ teaspoon dried basil

1 (28-ounce) can crushed tomatoes

Preparation

1 Preheat oven to 350 degrees F.

2 Cut bagel in half horizontally, then cut in half again (as shown in picture). Place bagel on baking sheet, cut side down. Spray bagel with cooking spray and sprinkle with cheese. Bake until cheese is just golden. Set aside.

3 Meanwhile, in a medium saucepan over medium heat, melt butter. Add onion and cook 3 to 4 minutes, or until softened, stirring occasionally. Sprinkle flour over onion and continue to cook 1 to 2 minutes, or until golden, stirring occasionally.

4 Slowly stir in milk, salt, pepper, sugar, and basil. Continue to cook 3 to 5 minutes, or until slightly thickened, stirring occasionally. Add tomatoes, reduce heat to low, and simmer 10 to 15 minutes, or until hot. Serve with warmed Parmesan dippers.

30 MINUTES OR LESS

Jewish Penicillin (Chicken Soup)

Ask six Jewish grandmothers what they think the secret to making great chicken soup is, and you'll probably get eight different answers. Some insist that it's all about adding parsnip, while others say ya can't forget the dill. So, we came up with a version that's perfect as is, but basic enough to add whatever "Bubbe" suggests. And if you're wondering why it's called "Jewish Penicillin," it's 'cause Jewish grandmas swear that their chicken soup can cure almost anything!

Serves 2

Ingredients

1 chicken leg quarter

1 carrot, cut into chunks

1 celery stalk, cut into chunks

¼ cup coarsely chopped onion

½ teaspoon salt

¼ teaspoon black pepper

5 cups water

1 to 2 teaspoons chicken base or 1 bouillon cube

1 cup cooked egg noodles

Preparation

1 In a soup pot over medium-high heat, add chicken, carrots, celery, onion, salt, pepper, and water; bring to a boil.

2 Reduce heat to low and simmer about 1 hour, or until chicken begins to fall off the bone. With a pair of tongs, carefully remove chicken, and place on a plate to cool slightly. Separate chicken from bones and skin. Cut chicken into chunks and return to pot. Discard bones and skin.

3 Add chicken base and stir until completely dissolved. Serve in bowls, over noodles.

Test Kitchen Tip: *If you're not sure what chicken base is, it's simply bouillon in the form of a paste, with a richer taste. You can find it in any market right next to the bouillon.*

5-Star Gazpacho

Not all soups are meant to be warm and cozy. Some, like gazpacho, are meant to be served chilled and are refreshing enough to be eaten on hot summer days. Luckily, this soup, which is typically served at fancy restaurants, can be made using off-the-shelf ingredients, like plain ol' tomato juice and a few veggies. Our version deserves a 5-star rating for how easy and tasty it is!

Serves 2

Ingredients

1-½ cups tomato juice

¼ cup diced cucumber

¼ cup diced green bell pepper

1 scallion, sliced

1 garlic clove, finely chopped

2 tablespoons red wine vinegar

1 tablespoon olive oil

½ teaspoon salt

1 teaspoon Worcestershire sauce

Preparation

1 In a large bowl, combine all ingredients. Serve chilled.

   Note: If you'd like, you can always use a regular or spicy vegetable juice in place of the tomato juice.

The Finishing Touch: *What do you say we garnish each serving with a jumbo shrimp to make dinner feel extra special? For less than the cost of a cup of coffee, we can turn simple gazpacho into a gourmet treat.*

30 MINUTES OR LESS

Chuck Wagon Beef Stew

Ok, we'll admit it—this beef stew was not created in a chuck wagon, nor was it a recipe that was passed down from Billy the Kid. It is, however, one of the best beef stews we've ever made. The reason we named it after the chuck wagon was that each spoonful paints a picture of a simpler time. Yes, it's comfort at its best.

Serves 2

Ingredients

½ pound boneless beef chuck roast or steak, cut into 1-inch cubes

½ teaspoon salt

¼ teaspoon black pepper

1 tablespoon vegetable oil

½ onion, cut into wedges

2 potatoes, peeled and cut into 1-inch chunks

2 carrots, cut into 1-inch chunks

½ teaspoon dried thyme

1-¾ cups beef broth

1-¼ cups water, divided

2 tablespoons all-purpose flour

½ teaspoon browning and seasoning sauce

Preparation

1 Season beef with salt and pepper.

2 In a large saucepan over high heat, heat oil until hot. Add beef and onion and cook 6 to 8 minutes, or until beef is well browned, stirring often.

3 Add potatoes, carrots, thyme, broth, and 1 cup water. Bring to a boil, cover, reduce heat to medium-low, and cook 40 to 45 minutes, or until meat and vegetables are tender.

4 In a small bowl, combine remaining ¼ cup water, the flour, and browning and seasoning sauce. Stir flour mixture into stew and cook uncovered 4 to 5 minutes, or until thickened.

Test Kitchen Tip: *To give our soups and stews a richer color, we like to add a bit of browning and seasoning sauce. You can typically find this ingredient in the spice aisle or near the steak sauces.*

State Fair Sausage Stew

There's no way to walk past the stand at the fair that sells sausage sandwiches and not be tempted to stop. The aroma of them cooking, along with all the peppers and onions, is almost too good to be true. Rather than waiting for the fair to return, you can make a pint-sized pot of stew that brings back all those fond memories. Maybe make some fried dough for dessert and let the fair festivities begin!

Serves 2

Ingredients

- 2 tablespoons vegetable oil
- ¾ pound Italian sausage, casing removed
- 1 green bell pepper, cut into 1-inch chunks
- 1 small onion, cut into 1-inch chunks
- 1 (14.5-ounce) can diced tomatoes
- 1 (8-ounce) can tomato sauce
- 1 clove garlic, minced
- ½ teaspoon Italian seasoning
- ¼ teaspoon salt
- ⅛ teaspoon black pepper

Preparation

1 In a large skillet over medium-high heat, heat oil until hot. Add sausage, pepper, and onion, and cook 6 to 8 minutes, or until sausage is browned.

2 Add the remaining ingredients, reduce heat to medium, and cook 10 to 15 minutes, or until tomatoes have broken down, stirring occasionally.

Serving Suggestion: *We suggest you have a loaf of crusty French bread on hand so you can sop up all the goodness. If you do a good enough job, ya might not even have to wash the dishes.*

All-American Chili

No matter where ya go in the country, everyone's got their own rules for making chili. In Cincinnati, they add cocoa powder to give it a rich taste. In Texas, they would never dream of adding beans (see page 84), and in California, they're pretty likely to lighten it up by using ground turkey instead of beef. All we know is, no matter where in the country you're from, everyone will appreciate the flavors of this good old American chili.

Serves 2

Ingredients

½ pound ground beef

¾ cup chopped onion

1 (15-ounce) can kidney beans, undrained

1 (15-ounce) can diced tomatoes, undrained

1 (8-ounce) can tomato sauce

1 tablespoon chili powder

1 teaspoon ground cumin

½ teaspoon salt

¼ teaspoon black pepper

Preparation

1 In a large saucepan over medium-high heat, cook ground beef and onion 4 to 6 minutes, breaking up beef as it cooks, until well browned, stirring occasionally.

2 Add remaining ingredients, reduce heat to low, stir until everything is well combined, then cover. Simmer 30 to 40 minutes, or until chili is thickened and all the flavors are blended, stirring occasionally.

Finishing Touch: Top each bowl of chili with some cheddar cheese and scallions to really take this over the top.

Patty's Blonde Chicken Chili

Our favorite blonde in the Test Kitchen, Patty, came up with this chili recipe that's not only downright tasty, but it's also perfect for a change-of-pace meal for two. It's made with just the right amount of chicken, beans, and veggies, to fill you up without having any go to waste. Kudos to Patty, yet again, for whipping up another delicious dish!

Serves 2

Ingredients

1 tablespoon vegetable oil

1 boneless, skinless chicken breast, cut into 1-inch cubes

¼ teaspoon salt

¼ teaspoon black pepper

½ cup chopped onion

1 clove garlic, minced

1 (15.5-ounce) can Great Northern beans, undrained

1 cup diced tomatoes

1-½ cups chicken broth

½ teaspoon ground cumin

½ teaspoon chili powder

Preparation

1 In a large saucepan over medium heat, heat oil until hot. Season chicken with salt and pepper, and sauté 5 to 6 minutes, or until golden. Add onion and garlic and cook 3 to 4 minutes, or until onion is tender.

2 Add remaining ingredients and bring to a boil. Reduce heat to low and simmer 30 to 35 minutes, or until chili thickens slightly, stirring occasionally.

Change it Up! *If ya don't have Great Northern beans, no problem! You can always use cannellini beans or any other white beans you already have in your pantry. After all, it's chili – anything goes!*

Texas-Style Chili

Put beans in a Texas-style chili and there's a pretty good chance you're gonna get a pan thrown at ya. Okay, we're kidding...maybe. Truth is, if you ask a real Texan what goes into their chili, they're going to say it's all about the beef. That's why we simmer plenty of beef with a whole lot of seasonings until it's tender-delicious. Then, you just put on a George Strait song and go to town!

Serves 2

Ingredients

2 tablespoons vegetable oil

1 pound lean beef chuck roast, cut into 1-inch cubes

¾ cup chopped onion

3 cloves garlic, minced

2 tablespoons chili powder

2 teaspoons ground cumin

¾ teaspoon salt

1 teaspoon hot pepper sauce

1 [8-ounce] can tomato sauce

1 cup water

2 tablespoons canned chopped green chilies

Preparation

1 In a large saucepan over medium-high heat, heat oil until hot. Add beef and cook 4 to 5 minutes, or until well browned. Drain off liquid, then add onion and garlic and sauté 5 minutes, or until onion is tender, stirring frequently.

2 Stir in chili powder, cumin, salt, and hot pepper sauce; cook 1 minute. Add tomato sauce, water, and chilies and bring to a boil, stirring occasionally. Reduce heat to low, cover, and simmer 30 to 35 minutes, or until beef is fork-tender.

Serving Suggestion: *We suggest serving this with a few slices of jalapeño and some corn chips.*

Pleasing Poultry

Crispy-Crunchy Oven-Fried Chicken

Who can resist fried chicken, especially when it's super crispy on the outside and moist 'n' juicy on the inside? Unfortunately, making it at home can be kind of messy and frying adds a whole lot of extra calories ya don't really want. That's why we came up with an easy and flavorful "oven-fried" version that delivers the same crunch we all love, without all the mess and guilt.

Serves 2

Ingredients

3 cups cornflake cereal, finely crushed

¾ teaspoon poultry seasoning

¼ teaspoon salt

⅛ teaspoon black pepper

⅛ teaspoon cayenne pepper (optional)

1 egg

2 teaspoons water

½ (3- to 4-pound) chicken, cut into 4 pieces (See Tip)

Cooking spray

Preparation

1 Preheat oven to 400 degrees F. Coat a baking sheet with cooking spray.

2 In a shallow dish, combine cereal, poultry seasoning, salt, black pepper, and cayenne pepper, if desired. In another shallow dish, whisk egg and water.

3 Dip chicken into egg mixture, then into cereal mixture, coating evenly on all sides. Place on baking sheet, then spray the chicken with cooking spray. (Yes, you spray the chicken. That's what makes it extra crispy.)

4 Bake 40 to 45 minutes, or until chicken is no longer pink in center and the coating is crispy.

Test Kitchen Tip: *If you can't find 1/2 of a chicken in the meat case, no problem! Just ask the butcher. And, depending on whether you like white or dark meat, feel free to mix and match breasts, wings, legs, thighs...you get the idea!*

Cowboy Roasted Chicken

Okay, so we didn't travel all the way to the Wild West to get this recipe, but we did get our inspiration from the cowboys of yesteryear. Ya see, they were big on cooking with lots of flavors, just like the ones we use in this recipe. The tempting aroma might just make you want to pull on your boots, saddle up a horse, and become a lasso-wielding cowboy.

Serves 2

Ingredients

- 1 (2-½- to 3-pound) chicken
- 2 tablespoons vegetable oil
- 1 teaspoon chili powder
- ½ teaspoon ground cumin
- ½ teaspoon onion powder
- ½ teaspoon salt
- ¼ teaspoon black pepper
- 3 cloves garlic, slivered

Preparation

1 Preheat oven to 350 degrees F. Remove giblets and neck from cavity of chicken (if necessary) and rinse with cold water. Dry well with paper towel. This will make the skin extra crispy. (See Tip)

2 In a small bowl, combine remaining ingredients; mix well. Place chicken in a roasting pan and rub spice mixture evenly over chicken. If any of the slivered garlic slides off, place it back on the chicken, (so we don't lose any of its deliciousness).

3 Bake 55 to 60 minutes, or until the juices run clear and the internal temperature is 165 degrees F.

Test Kitchen Tip: *Wanna have your Cowboy Roasted Chicken looking picture perfect? If so, dress it. No, not with bootcut jeans or a cowboy hat! Dressing a chicken means getting it ready for cooking. Here, we tucked the tips of the wings back under the breast and tied the drumsticks together with twine.*

One-Pan Chicken 'n' Rice

We're all looking for shortcuts when it comes to dinner—right? Of course we are! That's why we love this recipe. Ya see, since the rice and chicken are cooked all in one pan, this dish is just as easy to put together as it is to clean up. And don't let all that simplicity fool ya—there's creamy goodness in every bite.

Serves 2

Ingredients

1 cup water

½ cup uncooked long grain rice

½ cup diced tomato

½ (10-¾-ounce) can condensed cheddar cheese soup

¼ cup finely chopped onion

½ teaspoon garlic powder

¾ teaspoon dried thyme, divided

2 tablespoons vegetable oil

½ teaspoon salt

¼ teaspoon black pepper

6 chicken drumsticks (about 2 pounds)

Preparation

1 Preheat oven to 375 degrees F. Coat a 3-quart baking dish with cooking spray.

2 In the baking dish, combine water, rice, tomato, soup (see Tip), onion, garlic powder, and ¼ teaspoon thyme.

3 In a medium bowl, combine oil, salt, pepper, and remaining ½ teaspoon thyme. Add drumsticks to bowl and toss until evenly coated. Place over rice mixture.

4 Bake, covered, 25 minutes, then uncover and bake another 20 to 25 minutes, or until chicken is no longer pink in center and the rice is tender.

Test Kitchen Tip: *The other half of that can of cheddar cheese soup doesn't have to go to waste! Save it to make a great cheese sauce the next time you're serving veggies. Freeze in an airtight container until you're ready for it. Then, just defrost, pour into a bowl, add a little milk, warm it up in the microwave, and drizzle away!*

Roasted Honey Garlic Wings

Just the two of you sitting down to watch the big game tonight? This recipe makes just enough wings for twenty sticky fingers, if ya get what we mean. These taste extra-good, 'cause they're made from whole, fresh chicken wings, which are usually bigger than any you can get from your local take-out place. Plus, they're bathed in an amazing garlicky-honey glaze that'll make you forget you even set napkins out!

Makes 12

Ingredients

¼ cup vegetable oil

½ teaspoon salt

¼ teaspoon black pepper

1 dozen fresh chicken wings

½ cup honey

2 tablespoons chopped garlic

1 tablespoon
hot pepper sauce

Preparation

1 Preheat oven to 400 degrees F. In a large bowl, combine oil, salt, and pepper; add wings and toss until evenly coated. Place on rimmed baking sheet.

2 Bake 40 minutes; drain off excess liquid.

3 Meanwhile, in a small bowl, combine honey, garlic, and hot pepper sauce. Baste wings with sauce. Return to oven 15 to 20 additional minutes, or until no pink remains and juices run clear, basting occasionally.

Note: When we say wings, we mean the whole wing, not just the tip or the drumette. They'll be a welcome change.

Finishing Touch: *If you like your wings super saucy, we suggest you make an extra batch of the honey garlic sauce to serve on the side for dipping.*

Date-Night Chicken Supreme

Break out the candles and treat your special someone to a romantic evening for two by cooking up this mouthwatering main dish that looks as impressive as it tastes. (Don't worry, it's really easy to make!) Serve it with a side of roasted potatoes and a fresh veggie, and there's no telling what will happen. We've heard rumors that it's been the cause of many future dates...

Makes 2

Ingredients

- 2 boneless, skinless chicken breasts
- Salt and pepper for sprinkling
- 2 tablespoons garlic and herb cheese spread
- 2 thin slices deli ham
- 4 slices roasted red pepper
- 4 basil leaves
- 2 slices mozzarella cheese
- 1 tablespoon Parmesan cheese
- Paprika for sprinkling

Preparation

1 Preheat oven to 350 degrees F. Coat a rimmed baking sheet with cooking spray. Place chicken breasts on a cutting board and, with a sharp knife, cut each breast in half horizontally, cutting it only ¾ of the way through. (see Tip)

2 Open each breast like a book, then lightly sprinkle both sides with salt and pepper. Spread cheese evenly on half of each breast and top each with ham, roasted peppers, and basil. Fold over top half of each breast; place on baking sheet.

3 Bake 25 to 30 minutes, or until chicken is no longer pink in center. Top each breast with a slice of mozzarella cheese, sprinkle with Parmesan cheese and paprika, and bake 5 more minutes, or until cheese is melted. Serve immediately.

Test Kitchen Tip: *If you want to watch our how-to video on butterflying a chicken breast, visit MrFood.com and type "butterfly" in the search bar.*

Restaurant-Style Chicken Francaise

This chicken dish may have a fancy, French-sounding name, but its origins are actually Italian-American. Nowadays, you can find some version of this dish on the menu of almost any nice restaurant. Fork-tender and packed with fresh lemony flavor, it's no wonder why this dish is so popular. You'll love it 'cause it's tasty and filling, without making you feel stuffed.

Serves 2

Ingredients

¼ cup all-purpose flour

¼ teaspoon salt

¼ teaspoon black pepper

1 egg

2 teaspoons water

2 tablespoons butter, divided

2 boneless, skinless chicken breasts, pounded to ¼-inch thickness (see Tip)

⅓ cup white wine or dry vermouth

2 tablespoons lemon juice

1 teaspoon chopped fresh parsley

Preparation

1 In a shallow dish, combine flour, salt, and pepper; mix well. In another shallow dish, beat egg and water.

2 In a large skillet over medium heat, melt 1 tablespoon butter. Cut each piece of chicken in two. Dip chicken in flour mixture, then in egg, coating completely. Sauté chicken 4 to 5 minutes per side, or until golden; remove to a paper towel-lined platter.

3 Add remaining butter, the wine, lemon juice, and parsley to skillet; mix well, then return chicken to skillet. Cook 2 to 3 minutes, or until sauce begins to thicken and no pink remains in chicken. Serve chicken with sauce from pan.

Test Kitchen Tip: *Flattening a chicken breast is easy! First, place a towel on your counter and lay a cutting board on top of it. Then, place a chicken breast on the cutting board and cover with a gallon-size resealable plastic bag. With a meat mallet or a soup can, pound the chicken until desired thickness. If you're starting with really plump chicken breasts, try cutting them in half horizontally, and then go from there.*

30 MINUTES OR LESS

Jamaican Tipsy Chicken

Take your taste buds on a well-deserved vacation with this easy skillet chicken that's sure to make those long-day-stress-pains go away. You see, the chicken gets marinated in a mixture of island rum, lime, cream of coconut, and earthy spices, before it gets cooked to perfection. When it's time for serving, you may want to set the mood with some reggae music and a little rum punch. It's yummy, mon!

Serves 2

Ingredients

2 boneless, skinless chicken breasts, flattened slightly [See Tip page 98]

¼ cup light rum

¼ teaspoon ground nutmeg

1 tablespoon soy sauce

1 tablespoon lime juice

1 tablespoon brown sugar

⅛ teaspoon ground ginger

2 tablespoons butter

1-½ cups sliced fresh mushrooms

½ cup cream of coconut

Preparation

1 In a 9- x 13-inch glass baking dish, place chicken in a single layer; set aside.

2 In a small bowl, combine rum, nutmeg, soy sauce, lime juice, brown sugar, and ginger. Mix well and pour over chicken. Cover and refrigerate 1 hour, turning once.

3 In a large skillet or grill pan over medium heat, melt butter. Remove chicken from marinade, reserving excess marinade, and sauté chicken until no pink remains. Remove chicken to a serving platter and keep warm.

4 Add mushrooms and reserved marinade to pan and cook 3 to 5 minutes, or until mushrooms are tender. Stir in cream of coconut. Cook sauce over low heat 5 to 6 minutes, or until the sauce starts to thicken; serve over chicken.

Test Kitchen Tip:. *If you'd rather not use the rum, you can always substitute with a tablespoon of rum extract. And if you're stuck on what to do with that remaining cream of coconut, how about blending it with some rum, a small can of crushed pineapple, and ice to make a creamy tropical drink.*

30-Minute Chicken Cacciatore

When we looked at several other versions of chicken cacciatore to see what made them so special, one thing we noticed was how they all seemed to take hours to make. That may be great if we have nothing but time on our hands, but when we're cooking for two, we often want to make a great meal in about 30 minutes or less. So, after tweaking this and tweaking that, we came up with this quick version that has a long-cooked taste.

Serves 2

Ingredients

¼ cup all-purpose flour

½ teaspoon salt, divided

¼ teaspoon black pepper

2 boneless, skinless chicken breasts, cut into 1-inch chunks

2 tablespoons vegetable oil

1-½ cups quartered fresh mushrooms

1 green bell pepper, cut into 1-inch chunks

1 onion, cut into 1-inch chunks

2 cloves garlic, minced

1 (24-ounce) jar spaghetti sauce

1 cup water

1 teaspoon Italian seasoning

Preparation

1 In a shallow dish, combine flour, ¼ teaspoon salt, and the pepper. Toss chicken in flour mixture, coating completely.

2 In a soup pot over high heat, heat oil until hot; brown chicken on all sides, about 5 minutes. Remove chicken from pot; set aside.

3 Add mushrooms, green pepper, onion, and garlic to pot and cook 5 minutes, or until veggies are tender, stirring occasionally. Add remaining ingredients, including remaining ¼ teaspoon salt; return chicken to pot and bring to a boil. Reduce heat to low and simmer 15 to 20 minutes, allowing flavors to "marry," stirring occasionally.

Serving Suggestions: *Since this sauce is so yummy, we suggest you serve this over some curly egg noodles, to sop up all the goodness. And if your basil plant is brimming with leaves, feel free to snip some and use as a fresh and tasty garnish.*

30 MINUTES OR LESS

Sizzling-Hot Chicken Fajitas

Have you ever found yourself sitting in a restaurant and staring at the menu, trying to decide what to order, when a waiter walks by with a platter full of sizzling fajitas? After one sniff of the incredible aroma and a glimpse of all that sizzling meat and veggies, there's no question...you're ordering fajitas. With this simple version, you can get those same stimulating results right at home.

Serves 2

Ingredients

2 teaspoons ground cumin

2 teaspoons chili powder

½ teaspoon garlic powder

½ teaspoon salt

¼ teaspoon black pepper

2 boneless, skinless chicken breasts, cut into strips

4 (8-inch) flour tortillas

1 tablespoon vegetable oil

1-½ cups thinly sliced bell pepper (any color)

1 small onion, sliced

1 tablespoon lime juice

Preparation

1 In a large resealable plastic bag, combine cumin, chili powder, garlic powder, salt, and black pepper. Add chicken; seal and shake to coat.

2 Heat tortillas according to package directions; keep warm.

3 In a large skillet, heat oil until hot. Add chicken, discarding excess seasoning mixture, and cook 2 minutes, stirring occasionally. Add peppers and onions, stirring occasionally. When chicken is cooked through and the vegetables are tender, remove from heat. Stir in lime juice.

4 Place chicken mixture on a serving platter along with the warmed tortillas, so both of you can make your own.

Finishing Touch: *Don't forget to set out the toppings, so you can each make them your own. Some of our favorites are sour cream, guacamole, shredded cheese, and salsa.*

30 MINUTES OR LESS

Sweet 'n' Crunchy Chicken Fingers

We first tried this breading on salmon years ago, when a chef and good friend shared it with us. He actually served it at his high-end restaurant in New York, where everyone loved the sweet 'n' crunchy taste the breading added to their meal. The funny thing is, his customers never knew that this fancy-tasting breading actually started off with his kid's favorite breakfast cereal. Go figure!

Makes 6 to 8 strips

Ingredients

½ cup finely crushed sweetened corn and oat cereal (we used Cap'n Crunch)

¼ cup finely crushed butter-flavored crackers

¼ cup finely chopped pistachio nuts

1 pound chicken tenders

Cooking spray

Preparation

1 Preheat oven to 375 degrees F. Coat a rimmed baking sheet with cooking spray.

2 In a shallow dish, combine cereal, crackers, and nuts; mix well.

3 Lightly coat chicken with cooking spray, then dip in cereal mixture, coating completely. Place on baking sheet, then lightly coat the chicken with cooking spray again. (It'll make it crispy.)

4 Bake 15 to 18 minutes, or until chicken is no longer pink.

Fancy It Up: *Let us assure you that these are tasty as-is, but if you want to take them to a whole new level, try serving them with some Thai chili sauce. All it takes is just a little drizzle of the sauce right before serving. And in case you aren't familiar with it, you can typically find it in the ethnic section of your market, right next to the sweet and sour sauce.*

30 MINUTES OR LESS

Homemade Chicken Crock-Pies

Mom may have perfected the family-sized version of this meal, but we've come up with the best cozy chicken pot pie for two, and it starts off with leftover cooked chicken and frozen veggies. When ya bring these to the table, all bubblin' hot and with a flaky crust, they're not gonna have any idea you started with cooked chicken. Who knows, maybe they'll think yours is better than Mom's after all.

Serves 2

Ingredients

1 sheet frozen puff pastry, thawed [½ of a 17-ounce package]

1-½ cups cooked chicken, cut into ½-inch chunks

1-½ cups frozen mixed vegetables, thawed

1 [12-ounce] jar chicken gravy

½ teaspoon onion powder

¼ teaspoon salt

¼ teaspoon black pepper

Preparation

1 Preheat oven to 400 degrees F. Coat 2 [2-cup] crocks or 1 [1-quart] baking dish with cooking spray.

2 Cut puff pastry to fit top of crocks or baking dish. [See Tip.] Place dough on a baking sheet and bake 15 to 17 minutes, or until puffy and golden.

3 Meanwhile, in a skillet over medium heat, combine remaining ingredients and cook 10 to 12 minutes, or until heated through. Spoon into crocks, top with puff pastry, and serve immediately.

Test Kitchen Tip: *The trick to cutting the pastry to the right size is to lay it out on a cutting board. Place crocks or baking dish on it, upside down, and cut around the opening. Place cut dough on baking sheet and bake as directed.*

30 MINUTES OR LESS

Naked Sweet 'n' Sour Chicken

Don't take your clothes off just yet! It's the chicken that's getting naked this time 'cause there's no breading covering this bird up! That's 'cause this dish doesn't need any breading to make it taste better. There's enough of that Asian-inspired, sweet 'n' sour flavor to make the chicken taste incredible as is. Just make sure you're generous with the sauce; it's good enough to make 'em want to lick their plates clean.

Serves 2

Ingredients

2 tablespoons vegetable oil

1 pound boneless, skinless chicken breasts, cut into 1-inch chunks

1 clove garlic, minced

2 tablespoons ketchup

1 tablespoon honey

1 tablespoon white vinegar

1 (6-ounce) can pineapple juice

1 (8-ounce) can pineapple chunks in juice, undrained

1 red bell pepper, cut into chunks

2 tablespoons soy sauce

1 tablespoon cornstarch

2 scallions, cut into 1-inch pieces

Preparation

1 In a large skillet over medium-high heat, heat oil until hot. Add chicken and garlic and cook 4 to 5 minutes, or until the chicken begins to turn golden, stirring occasionally.

2 Add ketchup, honey, vinegar, pineapple juice, pineapple chunks (juice and all), and the red pepper, stirring until well combined. Reduce heat to medium-low and simmer, stirring occasionally.

3 Meanwhile, in a small bowl, combine soy sauce and cornstarch; whisk until well mixed.

4 When the sauce begins to boil, slowly stir in the soy sauce mixture; cook 2 to 3 more minutes, or until the chicken is cooked through and sauce has thickened. Top with scallions and serve.

Serving Suggestion: *To make this a complete meal, serve this over some white or brown rice. Of course, any rice is fine, but our personal favorites for this dish are either basmati or jasmine.*

30 MINUTES OR LESS

Take-Out Fake-Out Chicken Fried Rice

Don't be surprised when ya serve 'em a plate and they start looking around for the take-out containers. It's just that our "fake-out" version of fried rice is so good, it's hard to believe that anyone can make it at home. You might even want to pick up a couple sets of chopsticks, 'cause there's a good chance this will become a frequently requested recipe.

Serves 2

Ingredients

1 tablespoon plus 1 teaspoon sesame oil, divided

1 egg, beaten

1 chicken breast, cut into ½-inch pieces

2 cloves garlic, minced

⅛ teaspoon black pepper

1-½ cups cooked long grain rice, chilled (see Note)

¾ cup frozen peas and carrots, thawed

1 scallion, sliced

2 tablespoons soy sauce

Preparation

1 In a large skillet or wok over high heat, heat 1 teaspoon oil until hot. Add egg and stir constantly until scrambled. Remove to a bowl, break into small pieces, and set aside.

2 Add remaining 1 tablespoon oil to skillet and heat until hot. Stir in chicken, garlic, and pepper, and cook 4 to 5 minutes, or until chicken is no longer pink. Add rice, and peas and carrots, and stir-fry 3 to 4 minutes, or until rice begins to get crispy. Add scallion, soy sauce, and egg to mixture, and cook 2 to 3 minutes, or until heated through. Serve immediately.

Note: We think this is best when you let the cooked rice chill before adding it to the skillet. That means leftover rice is perfect for this.

So Many Options: If you enjoy having a take-out night once a week, you can easily change things up by substituting the chicken with cubed ham, ground beef, or shrimp. Hey, you can even leave out the meat altogether for a yummy vegetarian-friendly version!

30 MINUTES OR LESS

All-in-One
Chicken 'n' Veggie Toss

When it comes to weeknight meals, we need 'em to be quick, easy, and of course, satisfying. With that said, we came up with a dish that fits that description to a T. Our all-in-one skillet can be ready for eating in about 10 minutes and is just the kind of hearty meal you crave at dinnertime. Be sure ya dog-ear this page – it'll make it easier to find the next time you two are stuck in a dinnertime rut!

Serves 2

Ingredients

1 tablespoon vegetable oil

1 cup sliced fresh mushrooms

1 cup halved cherry or grape tomatoes

1 cup fresh broccoli florets

1 clove garlic, minced

1 (10-½-ounce) can cream of chicken soup

½ cup milk

¼ teaspoon dried rosemary

¼ teaspoon salt

⅛ teaspoon black pepper

1-½ cups cooked chicken, cut into 1-inch chunks

2 cups wide homestyle egg noodles, cooked according to package directions

1 tablespoon bacon bits

Preparation

1 In a large skillet over medium heat, heat oil until hot. Add mushrooms, tomatoes, broccoli, and garlic, and cook 5 minutes, or until tender.

2 Stir in soup, milk, rosemary, salt, pepper, and chicken, and heat 6 to 8 minutes, or until heated through.

3 Serve over warm noodles and sprinkle with bacon.

Serving Suggestion: *This recipe is great as is, but we think it's even better served with a little grated Parmesan cheese.*

Cornish Hens with Garlic and Rosemary

When Howard from the Test Kitchen first started his catering business years ago, serving Cornish hens was the "in" thing. What made these so popular, besides how darn cute they looked, was that everyone got their very own. So, just imagine the reaction you're gonna get when you serve up these pint-sized hens for a weeknight dinner. Who would ever think dinner for two could look so special?

Serves 2

Ingredients

3 tablespoons olive oil, divided

½ teaspoon salt

¼ teaspoon black pepper

2 Cornish hens, about 1 pound each, thawed if frozen

1 lemon, cut into wedges

2 sprigs fresh rosemary

10 cloves garlic

½ cup white wine or chicken broth

Preparation

1 Preheat oven to 350 degrees F. Coat a roasting pan with cooking spray.

2 In a small bowl, combine 2 tablespoons oil, the salt, and pepper; mix well. Place hens in roasting pan and rub seasoned oil over hens, coating completely. Place 1 lemon wedge, 1 sprig rosemary, and a garlic clove in the cavity of each hen. Place remaining lemon wedges and garlic cloves in pan around hens. Roast 30 minutes.

3 In a small bowl, whisk wine and remaining tablespoon oil; pour over hens. Continue roasting 30 to 40 more minutes, or until hens are golden brown and juices run clear, basting with pan juices every 10 minutes.

4 Remove hens to a platter, pouring any juices from the inside of each into the roasting pan. Pour pan juices, including the lemon and the garlic, into a small saucepan and simmer 4 to 5 minutes, or until it reduces and begins to thicken up. Serve hens immediately, drizzled with the flavor-packed sauce.

Turkey Meatloaf Florentine

When we first taste-tested this recipe around the Test Kitchen, everyone couldn't believe how moist and flavorful this was, considering it's made with ground turkey. Well, it took a lot of tries to get this just right, but we did it. The trick is to make sure there's plenty of seasoning and to include an ingredient that helps keep it moist, since turkey tends to be bland and a bit dry. Can you guess which ingredients do the trick here?

Makes 2

Ingredients

1 pound ground turkey

½ cup frozen chopped spinach, thawed, squeezed dry

¼ cup chopped onion

1 cup shredded mozzarella cheese

1 teaspoon garlic powder

½ teaspoon dried basil

½ teaspoon salt

¼ teaspoon black pepper

2 tablespoons water

Preparation

1 Preheat oven to 350 degrees F. Coat a rimmed baking sheet with cooking spray.

2 In a large bowl, combine all ingredients; mix well. Divide mixture in half and form into 2 individual loaves about 4 inches wide and 6 inches long. Place on baking sheet.

3 Bake 35 to 40 minutes, or until no pink remains and the internal temperature is 165 degrees F.

Stacked Thanksgiving Dinner for Two

How come it seems that after Thanksgiving, we always say how much we love turkey and all the trimmings, yet we don't really serve them again for another year? It must have to do with all the work that's involved in making a full Thanksgiving dinner. Well, this recipe makes it easy to have everything you love about that holiday meal, without all the work and cleanup. And it's so good, you won't have any leftovers to worry about!

Serves 2

Ingredients

¾ cup water

3 tablespoons butter, divided

1-½ cups cornbread stuffing mix (½ of a 6-ounce box)

¼ cup dried cranberries

¼ cup all-purpose flour

¼ teaspoon salt

¼ teaspoon black pepper

1 tablespoon vegetable oil

4 turkey cutlets (about ¾ pound)

1 (12-ounce) jar turkey gravy

Preparation

1 In a small saucepan over medium heat, bring water and 2 tablespoons butter to a boil. Stir in stuffing mix and dried cranberries, cover, remove from heat, and let sit 5 minutes; fluff with a fork, cover, and set aside.

2 In a shallow dish, combine flour, salt, and pepper. In a large skillet over medium-high heat, heat oil and remaining 1 tablespoon butter. Place turkey cutlets in seasoned flour, coating evenly. Place in skillet and cook 2 to 3 minutes per side, or until no longer pink.

3 Meanwhile, in a small saucepan over low heat, warm gravy.

4 Place 1 cutlet on each of 2 serving plates. Top each with half the stuffing and then top with remaining cutlets. Pour gravy over turkey and serve immediately.

30 MINUTES OR LESS

Bountiful Beef & Pork

Orange-Ginger Beef with Broccoli

Let's be honest—how many laps around the food court have you done just to keep getting samples of tasty orange beef served to you on a toothpick? We know we've done a few! Now, you don't have to work so hard to enjoy one of your favorite Asian flavors, and our version is better than the food court's. That's 'cause we stir-fry our beef with some broccoli and mandarin oranges in a homemade orange-ginger glaze that'll have you ditching the toothpick for a fork.

Serves 2

Ingredients

1 tablespoon vegetable oil

1 pound beef stir-fry meat

1 (11-ounce) can mandarin oranges, drained, with liquid reserved

¼ cup soy sauce

¼ cup honey

1 clove garlic, minced

¾ teaspoon ground ginger

1 tablespoon cornstarch

1 cup broccoli florets, thawed, if frozen

1 teaspoon sesame seeds (optional)

Preparation

1 In a large skillet over medium-high heat, heat oil until hot. Brown the beef, stirring occasionally.

2 Add liquid from mandarin oranges, the soy sauce, honey, garlic, and ginger; mix well. Reduce heat to medium-low, cover, and simmer 10 to 15 minutes, or until beef is tender, stirring occasionally.

3 In a small bowl, combine 2 tablespoons liquid from the skillet with the cornstarch. Stir in cornstarch mixture to skillet; simmer until sauce thickens. Gently stir in the oranges and the broccoli and continue to simmer until heated through. Sprinkle with sesame seeds, if desired, and serve immediately.

Test Kitchen Tip: *When cooking for two, we often end up tossing out produce that we don't use up before it goes bad. That's why in recipes like this we think frozen broccoli is the perfect solution. We just take out what we need and pop the rest back into the freezer until we need it again.*

30 MINUTES OR LESS

My Aunt's Italian Beef Roll-Ups

Kelly from our Test Kitchen loves Italian food, including her aunt's "braciola," which is basically a thin piece of beef rolled up with an incredible stuffing and simmered in a red sauce. So, when we made our version for her and got lots of "oohs" and "aahs" after just one bite, we knew we had hit the nail on the head. All that's missing is your own blend of TLC.

Serves 2

Ingredients

½ cup Italian-style bread crumbs

2 tablespoons grated Parmesan cheese

6 slices Genoa salami, chopped

1 egg

¼ teaspoon salt

¼ teaspoon black pepper

2 thin-cut top sirloin steaks (about 1 pound total)

2 tablespoons olive oil

2 cups spaghetti sauce

⅓ cup water

Preparation

1 In a small bowl, combine bread crumbs, cheese, salami, egg, salt, and pepper; mix well. Spread mixture evenly over the top of each steak; roll up jelly roll-style and secure each with a toothpick.

2 In a deep skillet over medium-high heat, heat oil until hot; brown beef rolls 5 to 6 minutes, or until browned on all sides.

3 Reduce heat to low and add spaghetti sauce and water; cover and simmer 25 to 30 minutes, or until beef is fork-tender. Remove toothpicks; slice as shown in photo, and serve with sauce.

Serving Suggestion: *If you're both cheese lovers, then go ahead and grab the Parmesan. You may even want to serve this with a side of pasta for an all-out Italian dinner.*

Braised Cola Short Ribs

You might want to think twice before you let them take that last can of cola out of the fridge! It just so happens to be the "secret ingredient" to making these short ribs so extraordinary. In fact, we wouldn't be surprised if it's what all the trendy restaurants and gourmet burger joints are using in their recipes. Now, who said you couldn't cook a trendy meal for two?

Serves 2

Ingredients

½ teaspoon garlic powder

½ teaspoon salt

½ teaspoon black pepper

2-½ to 3 pounds short ribs

2 tablespoons vegetable oil

1 cup regular cola beverage

1 cup chili sauce

1 tablespoon Worcestershire sauce

1 tablespoon hot pepper sauce

Preparation

1 In a small bowl, combine garlic powder, salt, and black pepper. Rub mixture over ribs.

2 In a large pot or Dutch oven over medium-high heat, heat oil until hot; brown ribs on all sides. Drain liquid from pot.

3 Meanwhile, in a medium bowl, combine remaining ingredients. Pour cola mixture over ribs. Reduce heat to medium, cover, and cook ribs 1-½ to 2 hours, or until fork-tender, turning and basting occasionally. Serve with pan drippings.

Fun Fact: The cola works double-duty in this recipe. First, it helps tenderize the short ribs as they slow cook. Second, it caramelizes, adding a rich flavor. You won't get that with diet cola, which is why we don't recommend a substitution.

Double Melt-Away Steak

A good steak is so tender it melts in your mouth, but a beyond-good steak features an herb butter topping that also melts with every bite. This is that steak. And if you finish yours in just minutes and reach over and grab their last bite...we don't blame you. Just watch out that you don't get your hand slapped.

Makes 2

Ingredients

½ stick (4 tablespoons) butter, softened

½ tablespoon Dijon mustard

1 teaspoon chopped fresh parsley

⅛ teaspoon plus ¼ teaspoon black pepper, divided

¼ teaspoon garlic powder

¼ teaspoon salt

2 New York strip steaks (about 1-½ pounds total)

Preparation

1 In a medium bowl, combine the butter, mustard, parsley, and ⅛ teaspoon black pepper. Mix until well blended, and set aside until ready to use.

2 In a small bowl, combine garlic powder, salt, and remaining ¼ teaspoon pepper; mix well. Season both sides of the steaks with the spice mixture.

3 Coat a grill pan or skillet with cooking spray and heat over medium-high heat until hot. Place steaks in pan and cook 4 to 5 minutes per side, or to desired doneness. Top each steak with a dollop of the herb butter. Let melt for a minute or so before digging in.

Serving Suggestion: *To give this more of a steakhouse experience, team it up with some thick-cut onion rings and creamed spinach. It doesn't get much better than that!*

30 MINUTES OR LESS

Smothered Sicilian Cubed Steak

There are a few ways to ensure that the beef you're making is super tender. The obvious way is to start off with premium cuts, but that can cost a fortune. Slow cooking is another good option too, but that requires lots of time. Using "cubed" or tenderized steak is typically the easiest and most inexpensive way. Good thing too, 'cause it's just what you need to make this melts-in-your-mouth Italian-style dinner.

Serves 2

Ingredients

3 tablespoons all-purpose flour

½ teaspoon paprika

½ teaspoon salt

¼ teaspoon black pepper

2 beef cubed steaks (about ¾ pound)

2 tablespoons olive oil

1 (14-½-ounce) can diced tomatoes, undrained

1-½ cups sliced fresh mushrooms

½ cup beef broth

1 teaspoon Italian seasoning

1 teaspoon garlic powder

½ tablespoon cornstarch

Preparation

1 In a shallow dish, combine flour, paprika, salt, and pepper; add steaks and turn to coat.

2 In a large skillet over medium-high heat, heat oil until hot. Cook steaks 8 to 12 minutes, or until no pink remains, turning halfway through cooking. Remove steaks to a platter and cover to keep warm.

3 Reduce heat to medium and add tomatoes, mushrooms, broth, Italian seasoning, and garlic powder. Cook 5 to 7 minutes, or until mushrooms are tender.

4 In a small bowl, combine 2 tablespoons liquid from skillet with cornstarch; stir until smooth. Slowly add back into the skillet and stir until smooth and thickened. Return steaks to skillet and cook until thoroughly heated. Serve each steak topped with sauce.

Decisions, Decisions: You can serve this with a heaping portion of penne pasta, or cut each steak in half lengthwise and pile it into a hoagie roll. Either way, when you top it with the sauce, you're in for some good eatin'.

30 MINUTES OR LESS

Super Juicy Roasted Prime Rib

There used to be a time when prime rib was something you'd only eat at fancy restaurants or on special occasions with the whole family. Not anymore! We've come up with a clever way to slow roast a juicy prime rib just for two. And if you love an end cut, which is usually the most sought-after piece, boy are you gonna love this!

Serves 2

Ingredients

1 tablespoon olive oil

½ teaspoon dried thyme leaves

½ teaspoon garlic powder

½ teaspoon salt

¼ teaspoon black pepper

1-½ to 1-¾ pound boneless ribeye (See Tip)

½ cup beef broth

¼ cup red wine

Preparation

1 Preheat oven to 350 degrees F. Place a roasting rack into a small roasting pan or baking dish and coat with cooking spray.

2 In a small bowl, combine oil, thyme, garlic powder, salt, and pepper; mix well. Heat a large skillet over medium-high heat until hot. Rub seasoning mixture over entire roast and place in skillet. Brown on all sides, then place on rack in roasting pan. Set skillet aside for deglazing later.

3 Roast 30 to 45 minutes for medium rare or until thermometer reaches 125 degrees F, or cook longer until desired doneness. Remove roast to a cutting board and let rest 10 minutes.

4 Meanwhile, to deglaze skillet, add broth and wine, and simmer 5 minutes. Slice roast in half and serve with sauce from skillet.

Test Kitchen Tip: *There's a pretty good chance you won't find a rib roast this small just waiting for you in the meat case. No problem though, just ask the butcher to cut you a boneless ribeye that is about 1-1/2 pounds. It's somewhere between a small roast and a thick ribeye.*

20-Minute Skillet Goulash

When Howard from our Test Kitchen was growing up, goulash was one of a few stand-by dinners his mom made on a regular basis. Since money was tight, it was a great way to feed the whole family for next to nothing. These days, he still makes it when he's craving comfort food and is pressed for time. The only difference is, he makes it just for two.

Serves 2

Ingredients

- 1 pound ground beef
- ¼ cup chopped onion
- 1-¼ cups beef broth
- 1 cup spaghetti sauce
- ¾ cup elbow macaroni
- ½ teaspoon garlic powder
- ½ teaspoon salt
- ¼ teaspoon black pepper
- ¼ cup shredded mozzarella cheese

Preparation

1 In a large skillet over high heat, brown ground beef and onion 5 to 7 minutes, or until no pink remains stirring frequently. Drain off excess liquid.

2 Add beef broth, spaghetti sauce, macaroni, garlic powder, salt, and black pepper; mix well. Cover, reduce heat to medium-low, and simmer 7 to 9 minutes, or until macaroni is tender.

3 Sprinkle with cheese and simmer 1 to 2 more minutes, or until cheese is melted.

Test Kitchen Tip: *Make sure you cover the pan when cooking the macaroni or it won't cook properly. And we don't know anyone who likes chewy pasta!*

Brown Sugar-Glazed Meatloaf

If you ate meatloaf for dinner at least a few times a month growing up, then, chances are, so did Mom and Grandma. Meatloaf is an American tradition that's been passed down from generation to generation, mostly 'cause it's just good ol' fashioned comfort food. For this recipe, we took the best part of many of our family-favorite meatloaves and created a version that's sized just-for-two.

Serves 2

Ingredients

1 pound ground beef

¼ cup finely chopped onion

¼ cup finely chopped green bell pepper

1 egg, beaten

⅓ cup Italian-style bread crumbs

3 tablespoons ketchup, divided

1 teaspoon garlic powder

½ teaspoon salt

¼ teaspoon black pepper

2 teaspoons brown sugar

Preparation

1 Preheat oven to 350 degrees F. Coat a rimmed baking sheet with cooking spray.

2 In a large bowl, combine ground beef, onion, green pepper, egg, bread crumbs, 2 tablespoons ketchup, the garlic powder, salt, and black pepper. Using your hands, gently mix ground beef mixture well, and form into a loaf shape on baking sheet.

3 Bake 30 minutes. Spoon on remaining tablespoon of ketchup and sprinkle with brown sugar. Bake 10 additional minutes, or until no pink remains and the brown sugar begins to caramelize. Slice and serve.

Test Kitchen Tip: To make sure your meatloaf is as juicy as can be, let it sit at least 10 minutes before slicing it; this will also ensure that it can be easily sliced. And depending on how big or small your appetites are, you might even have some leftovers, which would be perfect for sandwiches the next day.

Mini Minnesota Hot Dish

It doesn't matter where you live, this dinner favorite is as welcome as a gelatin mold at a church dinner, or deviled eggs at a Southern potluck. Not only is this dish super simple to make, 'cause it's baked in just one dish, but it's also a complete fill-ya-up meal. That's right, this two-rrific, all-in-one casserole features beef, veggies, and potatoes all baked together with a creamy base and a cheesy topping. Yum!

Serves 2

Ingredients

- 1 pound ground beef
- ¼ cup chopped onion
- ¼ teaspoon salt
- ⅛ teaspoon black pepper
- ½ (10-½-ounce) can cream of mushroom soup
- ¼ cup milk
- 1 cup frozen mixed vegetables, thawed
- ½ cup shredded cheddar cheese
- 1 cup frozen seasoned potato tots

Preparation

1. Preheat oven to 400 degrees F. Coat a 1-quart baking dish with cooking spray.

2. In a skillet over medium heat, brown ground beef, onion, salt, and pepper, stirring until meat crumbles and is no longer pink; drain. Spoon ground beef mixture into baking dish.

3. In a small bowl combine soup and milk; mix well. Stir in vegetables; pour vegetable mixture over meat. Sprinkle with cheese and top with potatoes.

4. Bake 30 to 35 minutes, or until potatoes are golden and casserole is heated through.

Beef 'n' Bean Enchilada Bake

You can fill an enchilada with practically anything, including beef, pork, chicken, seafood, and fresh veggies. With all of the tasty variations available, it was hard to choose just one recipe to share with you, but we finally settled on one tasty Tex-Mex combo: beef and beans. Lucky for you, this great- tasting enchilada bake is made with a few off-the-shelf shortcut ingredients, making it perfect for busy weeknights.

Serves 2

Ingredients

1 (10-ounce) can red enchilada sauce, divided

1 (10-½-ounce) can cream of mushroom soup

½ pound ground beef

1 (8.8-ounce) package pre-cooked Spanish rice, heated according to package directions

1 (9-ounce) can bean dip

4 (6-inch) flour tortillas

½ cup shredded pepper jack cheese

Preparation

1 Preheat oven to 350 degrees F. Coat an 8-inch square baking dish with cooking spray.

2 Place 2 tablespoons of the enchilada sauce in a small bowl and set aside. In a medium bowl, combine the rest of the enchilada sauce and the soup; mix well. Evenly spread 1 cup of the sauce mixture in baking dish; set aside.

3 In a skillet over medium heat, sauté beef until no longer pink; drain excess liquid, keeping the beef in skillet. Add rice, bean dip, and the 2 tablespoons of the enchilada sauce that was set aside; mix well.

4 Spoon an equal amount of mixture on center of each tortilla and roll up. Place seam side down in baking dish. Pour remaining sauce over tortillas and cover with aluminum foil.

5 Bake 35 minutes, remove from oven, sprinkle with cheese, and bake 5 to 10 additional minutes, or until cheese is melted.

Roasted Pork Tenderloin with Country Stuffing

Southern cooks will tell ya that you can dress up just about any dish with a good country-style stuffing. We know good advice when we hear it, so we followed suit by dressing up a juicy pork tenderloin with a flavorful seasoned stuffing. The results are one impressive dish that's fancy enough for date night and easy enough for weeknights.

Serves 2

Ingredients

1 (1-pound) pork tenderloin

2 tablespoons olive oil

2 cloves garlic, minced

¼ teaspoon onion powder

½ teaspoon salt

¼ teaspoon black pepper

1 (6-ounce) package pork stuffing mix, prepare ½ the package according to directions

Preparation

1 Preheat oven to 350 degrees F. Coat a baking sheet with cooking spray.

2 Place pork on baking sheet. Using a sharp knife, cut a slit lengthwise down the center of pork, about ¾ of the way through, being careful not to cut all the way through. (See photo.)

3 In a small bowl, combine oil, garlic, onion powder, salt, and pepper; mix well. Rub herb mixture over pork. Spoon the stuffing into the slit, packing lightly with your fingers.

4 Roast about 25 minutes, or until pork is medium (145 degrees F). Let rest 5 minutes, before cutting into ½-inch slices. Serve immediately

Serving Suggestion: *A dish like this goes great with a side of steamed country vegetables, like green beans or broccoli. You can add a few roasted cherry tomatoes for a pop of color, too!*

Cheese-Crusted Pork Kabobs

Sometimes by simply changing the way we serve something we can turn it into a whole new dish. Here, we took hand-trimmed pork chops and cut 'em into cubes to make tasty kabobs that are super fun to eat. The added bonus, aside from how good the yummy cheese breading is, is that these cook up in no time, making them perfect for extra-busy weeknights.

Serves 2

Ingredients

- 2 boneless pork loin chops (about 1 pound total)
- 1 cup cheese crackers, finely crushed
- 2 tablespoons Parmesan cheese
- 1 teaspoon chopped fresh parsley
- ¼ teaspoon salt
- ⅛ teaspoon black pepper
- 1 egg
- 4 (6- to 8-inch) skewers
- Cooking spray

Preparation

1. Preheat oven to 400 degrees F. Coat a rimmed baking sheet with cooking spray. Cut each pork chop into 6 equal chunks.

2. In a shallow bowl, combine cracker crumbs, Parmesan cheese, parsley, salt, and pepper; mix well. In another shallow bowl, beat egg.

3. Dip each piece of pork in beaten egg, then into the cracker mixture, coating well. Place 3 pieces of pork on each skewer, leaving a little space between pieces. Place skewers onto baking sheet and spray pork with cooking spray. (This will make the coating extra crispy.)

4. Bake 15 to 20 minutes until center is slightly pink, or until desired doneness.

Test Kitchen Tips: *If you're using wooden skewers, be sure to soak them in water for about 15 minutes before using, so they won't burn. And just a reminder, according to the USDA, pork can be cooked to a medium temperature, (145 degrees F) which may be a little different from how it was cooked in the past. You'll find this makes the pork so much juicier.*

30 MINUTES OR LESS

Country Pork Chops with Buttermilk Gravy

You may want to put a bib on, 'cause we've found that just reading this recipe can cause folks to start drooling uncontrollably. We understand it has something to do with dreaming about thick-cut, buttermilk-dipped pork chops, coated with a flavor-packed breading and pan-fried until crispy. But it could also be the old-fashioned buttermilk gravy that gets served on top. Either way, this is the kind of comfort food that you just can't get out of your mind.

Makes 2

Ingredients

⅛ teaspoon garlic powder

⅛ teaspoon onion powder

¼ teaspoon plus ⅛ teaspoon salt, divided

¼ teaspoon black pepper, divided

2 bone-in, thick-cut, center-cut pork chops

4 tablespoons all-purpose flour, divided

1 cup buttermilk, divided

1 tablespoon vegetable oil

Preparation

1 In a small bowl, combine garlic powder, onion powder, ¼ teaspoon salt, and ⅛ teaspoon pepper. Sprinkle seasoning mixture evenly on both sides of pork chops.

2 Place 3 tablespoons flour in a shallow dish. In another shallow dish, place ¼ cup buttermilk. Dip chops in buttermilk, then coat both sides with flour.

3 In a large skillet over medium heat, heat oil until hot; add chops and cook 5 to 6 minutes on each side, or until desired doneness and golden brown. Drain on paper towels and cover to keep warm.

4 Meanwhile, whisk the remaining tablespoon of flour into remaining buttermilk, along with remaining ⅛ teaspoon salt and ⅛ teaspoon pepper. Slowly stir the buttermilk mixture into the skillet and simmer over low heat until thickened, stirring constantly. Serve sauce over chops.

30 MINUTES OR LESS

Old World Overstuffed Peppers

In the Old World, a hearty meal consisted of a fill-ya-up starch, flavorful meat, and a rich-tomato based sauce. Grandmas from all over have been known to "overstuff" their grandkids with meals like this, and we love them all the more for it. So, we took some inspiration from "nonna" and overstuffed these peppers with some of her signature hearty flavors to make this meal that's perfectly sized for two.

Makes 2

Ingredients

½ pound bulk Italian sausage

½ cup uncooked orzo pasta

1 (15-ounce) can tomato sauce, divided

½ cup plus 1 tablespoon water, divided

¼ teaspoon dried basil

¼ teaspoon garlic powder

¼ teaspoon salt

¼ teaspoon black pepper

2 green bell peppers, tops removed, cored

Preparation

1 In a large bowl, crumble sausage. Add orzo, ½ cup tomato sauce, 1 tablespoon water, the basil, garlic powder, salt, and black pepper; mix well.

2 Stuff bell peppers evenly with mixture. Stand peppers in a saucepan and pour remaining tomato sauce over top. Pour remaining ½ cup water in bottom of saucepan.

3 Cover, and cook over medium-low heat 45 to 55 minutes, or until the filling is cooked through and peppers are tender.

Decisions, Decisions: *Peppers come in many different colors, so feel free to switch these up every now and then. Maybe you prefer a traditional green pepper, while your partner would rather have a milder red or yellow pepper.*

The Best Barbecue Ribs Ever

After making these just once, you're going to discover just how amazing they are, and you're going to want to bookmark this page, so you can make 'em over and over again. But even if you do forget to bookmark it, it'll be easy to find, since there's a pretty good chance the recipe will be covered with your barbecue sauce fingerprints. In our experience, it's those recipes that are splattered, tattered, and torn that are simply the best.

Serves 2

Ingredients

½ teaspoon paprika

½ teaspoon onion powder

½ teaspoon garlic powder

½ teaspoon salt

½ teaspoon black pepper

1 rack pork baby back ribs (about 2 pounds)

½ cup barbecue sauce

¼ cup honey

1 teaspoon hot sauce

Preparation

1 Preheat oven to 350 degrees F.

2 In a small bowl, combine paprika, onion powder, garlic powder, salt, and pepper. Rub mixture over ribs. Loosely wrap ribs in aluminum foil, leaving room for steam to circulate, and seal edges tightly. Place on baking sheet.

3 Roast 1-¾ hours, or until fork-tender. Meanwhile, in a medium bowl, combine barbecue sauce, honey, and hot sauce; mix well.

4 Open foil packet carefully...it'll be hot! Brush ribs with sauce, leave uncovered, and return to oven 15 to 20 minutes, or until sauce begins to caramelize.

Serving Suggestion: *If you like your ribs extra saucy, then we suggest making a double batch of the sauce. Use half the sauce for basting, and you'll still have plenty to slather on while eating 'em.*

Scalloped Potatoes & Ham Casserole

Casseroles like this are really popular after the holidays, 'cause they're typically put together using leftovers, but that shouldn't always be the case. Now, you can make a creamy dinner casserole for two any time the craving sets in! And since it's a complete meal that's baked in one pan, you can bet that cleanup is a breeze.

Serves 2

Ingredients

- ¾ pound fully cooked boneless ham, cut into ½-inch chunks
- 1 (20-ounce) package refrigerated shredded hash brown potatoes
- 1 (10-¾-ounce) can condensed cheddar cheese soup
- 1 cup frozen peas
- ¾ cup milk
- ½ teaspoon onion powder
- ¼ teaspoon salt
- ⅛ teaspoon black pepper

Preparation

1 Preheat oven to 350 degree F. Coat a 1-½-quart casserole dish with cooking spray.

2 In a large bowl, combine all ingredients; mix well, then pour into casserole dish and cover tightly with aluminum foil.

3 Bake 30 minutes, then uncover and bake 20 to 25 additional minutes, or until potatoes are tender and the top begins to get crispy.

Note: You can use leftover ham, buy a single ham steak, or ask the deli to give you a thick cut of ham and go from there.

Serving Suggestion: Okay, so this recipe could feed more than two at dinnertime, but we felt that it was so good that you'd definitely want some leftovers to take to work the next day. It warms up great in the microwave.

Sensational Seafood & Pasta

Jumbo Baked Stuffed Shrimp

Surprise your loved one with a gourmet-style dish that'll have them wondering whether you snuck a five-star chef into the kitchen. Jumbo shrimp are stuffed with lots of seasoned crabmeat before getting baked to golden perfection. Serve them with some baby roasted potatoes and you're set for a meal that's full of ooh-la-la without all the "too much work."

Serves 2

Ingredients

1 (6-ounce) can crabmeat, drained and flaked

3 tablespoons finely chopped celery

2 tablespoons plain bread crumbs

1 tablespoon mayonnaise

1 teaspoon lemon juice

½ teaspoon seafood seasoning (we used Old Bay)

½ pound jumbo raw shrimp, peeled, with tails on (about 8)

Paprika for sprinkling

Preparation

1 Preheat oven to 375 degrees F. Coat a baking sheet with cooking spray.

2 In a bowl, combine crabmeat, celery, bread crumbs, mayonnaise, lemon juice, and seafood seasoning; mix well.

3 Butterfly shrimp by cutting lengthwise along the outer curve, ¾ of the way through. Open the slit and devein. Mound a spoonful of crabmeat mixture in each opening, gently packing in the filling. Place on baking sheet and sprinkle with paprika.

4 Bake 7 to 10 minutes, or until shrimp turn pink. Serve immediately.

Test Kitchen Tip: *We used a can of crabmeat here, since it's just the right size, but if you'd rather use fresh lump crabmeat, feel free to swap it out. The choice is up to you!*

Sautéed Shrimp with Basil Cream Sauce

You can save the cocktail sauce for another shrimp recipe, 'cause these huge shrimp are swimming in their own flavor-packed cream sauce. The sauce is so good we had to serve these over toasted French bread, so you can sop up every last drop. And, as if it couldn't get any better, this restaurant-fancy dish is really weekday-easy.

Serves 2

Ingredients

½ stick (4 tablespoons) butter

2 tablespoons olive oil

½ pound raw extra-large shrimp, peeled and deveined

1 clove garlic, minced

2 tablespoons Dijon mustard

1-½ teaspoons Worcestershire sauce

⅛ teaspoon salt

⅛ teaspoon black pepper

¼ cup half-and-half

1 teaspoon lemon juice

2 tablespoons minced fresh basil leaves

4 slices French bread, toasted

Preparation

1 In a large skillet over medium heat, melt butter with oil until hot. Add shrimp and sauté 3 to 4 minutes or until pink, stirring occasionally. Remove to a plate and cover to keep warm.

2 In the same skillet, add garlic, Dijon mustard, Worcestershire sauce, salt and pepper; mix well. Slowly stir in half-and-half and cook until hot. Add shrimp, lemon juice, and basil to skillet and stir until evenly coated.

3 Spoon mixture over toasted bread and serve.

Did You Know? When buying shrimp, it's important to remember that the bigger the shrimp are, the less you'll get per pound. For example, extra-large shrimp usually have about 21 to 25 shrimp per pound, whereas medium shrimp usually have about 50 to 70 shrimp per pound. In this recipe you want to use bigger shrimp, so you really have something to bite into!

30 MINUTES OR LESS

Seared Scallops Over Angel Hair

We wanted big flavors and big portions when coming up with this recipe, which is why we used sea scallops (instead of the smaller bay scallops) to make this angelic-tasting, seafood pasta dish. Their larger size means you can enjoy more scallop in every bite, and that they'll soak up more of that buttery-herb and lemon mixture!

Serves 2

Ingredients

5 tablespoons butter, divided

1 tablespoon olive oil

¾ pound sea scallops, patted dry with a paper towel

¼ teaspoon salt, plus extra for sprinkling

⅛ teaspoon black pepper, plus extra for sprinkling

Paprika for sprinkling

¼ cup finely chopped onion

½ cup white wine

1 tablespoon fresh lemon juice

1 tablespoon chopped fresh parsley

1 teaspoon lemon zest

¼ pound angel hair pasta, cooked according to package directions

Preparation

1 In a large skillet over medium-high heat, melt 1 tablespoon butter with oil until hot. Sprinkle both sides of scallops with salt, pepper, and paprika. Place in hot skillet and sear 2 to 3 minutes per side, or until browned. Remove to a plate.

2 In the same skillet over medium heat, melt remaining 4 tablespoons butter and sauté onion 3 to 4 minutes, or until softened. Stir in wine, lemon juice, parsley, remaining ¼ teaspoon salt, and remaining ⅛ teaspoon black pepper, and heat until hot, stirring occasionally.

3 Add the scallops back to the skillet and heat just until hot. Sprinkle with lemon zest and serve over warm pasta.

Test Kitchen Tip: *If you've always shied away from making scallops at home because you weren't sure you could cook them properly, then we're going to let you in on the secret to perfect scallops every time: it's all about how dry you get 'em before you pan sear them. When they're dried well, they'll get a golden crust instead of becoming steamed. Oh, and make sure not to overcook 'em or they'll get tough and chewy!*

30 MINUTES OR LESS

Beer-Battered Fish Fry

The British love fish and chips as much as we love burgers and fries, and we don't blame 'em. The moment you first bite into the crunchy batter before reaching the super moist fish is absolutely unforgettable. And, believe it or not, what makes the batter taste so amazing is in another British favorite: beer. Ya see, the malt gives it a rich flavor and the tiny bubbles make the batter light and crispy. Serve with thick-cut fries ("chips") and enjoy, mates!

Serves 2

Ingredients

- ¾ cup pancake mix
- 1 teaspoon sugar
- ¼ teaspoon salt
- ⅓ cup beer
- 1 egg, beaten
- 1 cup vegetable oil for frying
- 1 pound cod or other white-fleshed fish fillets, cut into 4 pieces

Preparation

1 In a large bowl, combine pancake mix, sugar, salt, beer, and egg; mix well, but do not overmix.

2 In a large skillet over medium heat, heat oil until hot (350 degrees F). Dip fish into batter, coating completely, then fry 3 to 5 minutes per side, or until coating is golden and fish flakes easily with a fork.

3 Drain on a paper towel-lined platter. Serve immediately.

Test Kitchen Tip: *If you prefer to keep this non-alcoholic, feel free to use a non-alcoholic beer. And if your fish is super thin or super thick, the cooking time will vary.*

South-of-the-Border Fish Tacos

Fish tacos are a staple at just about any place that sells tacos. Gourmet restaurants serve them with funky toppings and you can always tell when a food truck is serving them, 'cause the line will wrap around the block. Our fish tacos are nothing less than spectacular, featuring the combo of tasty white fish, crunchy slaw, and a creamy cilantro sauce. Hands down, these are a winner.

Serves 2

Ingredients

- 2 tablespoons sour cream
- 2 tablespoons mayonnaise
- 1 tablespoon chopped fresh cilantro
- 1 (1.25-ounce) package taco seasoning mix, divided
- 1-½ cups shredded coleslaw
- 1 teaspoon apple cider vinegar
- ½ teaspoon sugar
- 2 tablespoons vegetable oil, divided
- 1 pound tilapia or other white-fleshed fish fillets, cut into 1-inch pieces
- 4 (6-inch) flour tortillas

Preparation

1 In a small bowl, combine the sour cream, mayonnaise, cilantro, and 2 teaspoons taco seasoning; mix well and set aside. In another small bowl, combine coleslaw, vinegar, sugar, and 1 tablespoon oil; toss until evenly coated.

2 In a medium bowl, mix the remaining 1 tablespoon oil and remaining taco seasoning. Add the fish and gently toss to coat.

3 Coat a medium skillet with cooking spray and over medium heat, cook fish 4 to 5 minutes, or until fish is firm to the touch.

4 Place fish evenly down the center of tortillas, then top with coleslaw and sour cream topping, and roll up.

Mediterranean Fish Bundles

Packet cooking isn't anything new. Fancy restaurants have been wrapping all sorts of ingredients in parchment paper for years, while the tropical tradition of using banana leaves to cook everything from pork to fish is decades-long. Today, you can recreate this cooking method at home with aluminum foil. The concept is the same: lock in the flavors and end up with super moist results. This tastes just as great whether ya make it in your oven or over an open fire!

Serves 2

Ingredients

2 cups fresh spinach

2 (6-ounce) tilapia fillets

½ teaspoon dried oregano

Salt for sprinkling

Black pepper for sprinkling

2 teaspoons lemon juice

¼ cup crumbled feta cheese

2 tablespoons sliced, pitted Kalamata olives

2 teaspoons olive oil

Preparation

1 Preheat oven to 375 degrees F. Tear off 2 pieces of aluminum foil about 12- x 18-inches each.

2 Evenly divide spinach on each piece of foil. Place a fish fillet on top of spinach. Sprinkle each with oregano, salt, and pepper. Drizzle with lemon juice. Evenly sprinkle with cheese and olives, and drizzle with oil. Bring edges of foil together, creating a packet, and seal.

3 Place foil-wrapped bundles on a rimmed baking sheet and bake 15 to 20 minutes, or until fish flakes easily with a fork.

Test Kitchen Tip: *Be careful when opening the foil bundles, as they'll be mighty hot and will release a burst of steam.*

Southern Catfish Fillets

We got "hooked" on catfish after visiting a few of the catfish farms deep in the South. It was fascinating to learn how catfish are harvested from fresh water farms, and how folks in the South have found so many different ways to eat this mild and fresh-tasting fish. Inspired by all that we saw, we came up with a simple Southern way of making catfish that's good enough to eat any day of the week.

Serves 2

Ingredients

- 1 egg
- 2 tablespoons mayonnaise
- ¼ teaspoon cayenne pepper, divided
- 2 teaspoons grated Parmesan cheese
- ¾ cup self-rising cornmeal
- ⅛ teaspoon salt
- ½ cup vegetable oil
- 2 catfish fillets (about 1 pound)

Preparation

1 In a shallow dish, whisk together the egg, mayonnaise, ⅛ teaspoon cayenne pepper, and Parmesan cheese. In another shallow dish, combine cornmeal, remaining ⅛ teaspoon cayenne pepper, and the salt; mix well.

2 In a large skillet over medium heat, heat oil until hot. Dip catfish in egg mixture, then in cornmeal mixture, coating completely.

3 Cook catfish in skillet for 3 to 4 minutes per side, or until coating is golden and fish flakes easily with a fork. Drain on a paper towel-lined platter, then serve.

Serving Suggestion: *Complete your meal with a few shortcut items from the freezer case. A package of frozen creamed spinach and some waffle-cut sweet potato fries are perfect go-alongs.*

30 MINUTES OR LESS

Honey-Dijon Roasted Salmon

Wild or farm-raised, salmon is a super versatile fish. In the Test Kitchen we've poached it, seared it, made burgers with it, and have even eaten it raw. No matter how we've prepared it, we've always gotten rave reviews. So, when we set out to come up with the perfect way to make salmon just for two, we knew we had some mighty high expectations to meet. We have to say, this is one salmon dish that's bound to be top-rated.

Serves 2

Ingredients

2 salmon fillets
(about ¾ pound total)

Salt for sprinkling

Black pepper for sprinkling

2 tablespoons honey

1-½ teaspoons Dijon mustard

1 clove garlic, minced

Preparation

1 Preheat oven to 350 degrees F. Coat a baking sheet with cooking spray.

2 Place salmon fillets on baking sheet. Lightly sprinkle with salt and pepper. In a small bowl, combine honey, mustard, and garlic; mix well. Spoon mixture evenly over each fillet.

3 Bake 15 to 20 minutes, or until fish flakes easily.

Test Kitchen Tip: *Make cleanup a breeze by lining your pan with foil. We've found it's a lot easier to throw away the foil than it is removing the caramelized glaze off your pan. We learned that the hard way!*

30 MINUTES OR LESS

My Grandmother's Tuna Croquettes

Howard, from our Test Kitchen, has fond memories of his grandma serving these alongside a pot of her "almost-famous" pea soup. She'd serve them to everybody who'd come over, and always with a sweet smile on her face. It was the pleasure of seeing how much her guests enjoyed these simple croquettes that brought her such joy. This is one of those dishes that's good whether you're the one making 'em or being served.

Serves 2

Ingredients

1 (12-ounce) can tuna in water, drained and flaked

2 scallions, thinly sliced

½ cup Italian-style bread crumbs

1 tablespoon grated Parmesan cheese

1 egg, lightly beaten

½ teaspoon garlic powder

¼ teaspoon salt

⅛ teaspoon black pepper

1 tablespoon vegetable oil

Preparation

1 In a medium bowl, combine tuna, scallions, bread crumbs, Parmesan cheese, egg, garlic powder, salt, and pepper; mix well. Shape mixture into 4 patties.

2 In a large skillet over medium heat, heat oil until hot. Cook patties 4 to 5 minutes per side, or until golden brown. Serve immediately.

Finishing Touch: *As good as these are on their own, you can make 'em even better by whipping up a creamy sauce to serve them with. For that, all you do is combine 1 tablespoon mayonnaise, 1 tablespoon sour cream, 1 teaspoon hot sauce, ½ teaspoon Worcestershire sauce, ¼ teaspoon garlic powder, and ⅛ teaspoon salt in a small bowl. Give it a good stir and it's ready to serve!*

30 MINUTES OR LESS

Truly Unbelievable Mac 'n' Cheese

There's no going back to the blue box when you make this homemade mac 'n' cheese for two. This from-scratch version is extra creamy and made with sharp Cheddar, so you know there's lots of bold cheesy flavor. Plus, we like to top ours with a cracker crumb mixture that adds a tasty crunch.

Serves 2

Ingredients

5 tablespoons butter, divided

¼ cup all-purpose flour

½ teaspoon dried mustard

½ teaspoon salt

¼ teaspoon black pepper

1-¼ cups milk

1-½ cups shredded sharp cheddar cheese

½ pound elbow macaroni, cooked according to package directions

½ cup crushed saltine crackers

Preparation

1 Preheat oven to 375 degrees F. Coat 2 (2-cup) ramekins or a 1-½-quart baking dish with cooking spray.

2 In a large saucepan over medium heat, melt 4 tablespoons butter. Add flour, dried mustard, salt, and pepper; mix well. Gradually stir in milk, bring to a boil, and cook until thickened, stirring constantly. Add cheese and continue stirring until melted. Add macaroni to cheese sauce; mix well. Spoon mixture into ramekins.

3 In a microwave-safe bowl, melt remaining 1 tablespoon butter in microwave. Stir in cracker crumbs and mix until evenly coated. Sprinkle crumb mixture evenly over macaroni.

4 Bake 30 to 35 minutes, or until bubbly and golden brown.

So Many Options: *If you open your fridge and you've got all kinds of cheese except, of course, Cheddar, no problem! Feel free to mix and match. The only cheeses we don't recommend using are blue or mozzarella, which can make the sauce a little stringy.*

Mamma Mia Skillet Lasagna

Everyone knows there's nothing like homemade lasagna, but we also know that it can take an entire Sunday afternoon to make a great one from scratch, and when we're done we end up with enough to feed the whole block. We're not willing to pass up everything we love about lasagna, so we came up with a skillet version that's ideal for the two of you, and promises to leave you saying, "Mamma Mia! That was good!"

Serves 2

Ingredients

6 lasagna noodles, broken into 2-inch pieces

½ pound ground beef

1 teaspoon minced garlic

2 cups spaghetti sauce

1 cup shredded mozzarella cheese

¼ cup ricotta cheese

1 teaspoon chopped fresh basil

Preparation

1 Cook noodles according to package directions; drain and set aside.

2 In a large skillet over medium heat, brown ground beef; drain excess liquid.

3 Add garlic and spaghetti sauce to skillet; reduce heat to medium and cook 3 to 5 minutes, or until hot. Gently stir in cooked noodles and simmer 3 minutes. Sprinkle with mozzarella cheese and heat until cheese is melted.

4 Dollop with ricotta cheese, sprinkle basil over the top, and serve.

So Many Options: We love this dish so much we've made it many times. A few times, when we were out of lasagna noodles, we've made it with bow tie pasta, and....guess what? It tastes just as good!

30 MINUTES OR LESS

Northern Italian Ravioli Bake

It may be hard to believe, but not all Italians cook with lots of tomato sauce. Northern Italians prefer to use cream-based sauces and plenty of cheese in their dishes. We think all of Italy's dishes are "molto bene!" (very good!), but for this recipe for two we turned to the northerners for inspiration. We have a feeling you're going to love the creamy and cheesy goodness of this pasta bake just as much as we do.

Serves 2

Ingredients

1-½ cups Alfredo sauce

½ cup frozen chopped spinach, thawed, squeezed dry

1 pound frozen cheese ravioli

2 teaspoons grated Parmesan cheese

1 cup shredded mozzarella cheese

Preparation

1   Preheat oven to 375 degrees F. Spread ½ cup Alfredo sauce on bottom of a 1-½-quart baking dish. Evenly distribute ½ the spinach over sauce, layer ½ the ravioli on next, then sprinkle with 1 teaspoon Parmesan cheese. Pour ½ cup Alfredo sauce on top, then evenly sprinkle ½ cup mozzarella cheese. Repeat layers 1 more time, ending with sauce.

2   Cover and bake 40 to 45 minutes, or until hot in center. Remove cover and sprinkle with remaining ½ cup mozzarella cheese. Bake 5 more minutes, or until cheese is melted and starts to turn golden.

Test Kitchen Tip: *The nice thing about this dish is how easy it is to change up. Instead of using ravioli stuffed with cheese, you can try ravioli stuffed with meat, lobster, or veggies. Maybe you could try a different one every time?*

Everything-in-One-Pot Pasta

Give the dishwasher a break and make this pasta dish that cooks up in just one pot. Yup, that means no pre-cooking the pasta in a separate pot before combining the rest of your ingredients! This tomato and herb pasta dinner is more than just great, it's "supercalifragilisticexpialidocious" (that's fantastic in layman's terms!). Good thing it takes less time to make than it does to say how good it tastes.

Serves 2

Ingredients

8 ounces linguine, uncooked, broken in half

1 (14.5-ounce) can diced tomatoes, undrained

½ onion, thinly sliced

2 cloves garlic, thinly sliced

2 cups chicken broth

1 teaspoon dried oregano

¼ teaspoon salt

1 tablespoon olive oil

1 tablespoon chopped fresh basil

Parmesan cheese for garnish

Preparation

1 In a large saucepan, place linguine, tomatoes, onion, and garlic. Pour in chicken broth and sprinkle with oregano and salt. Drizzle oil on top and cover.

2 Bring to a boil over medium-high heat, then reduce heat to low and simmer 15 minutes, stirring every 2 to 3 minutes, or until liquid is almost gone.

3 Garnish with basil and Parmesan cheese; serve immediately.

Did You Know? *The trick to cooking the pasta in this recipe is making sure that there's enough liquid in the sauce to allow the pasta to cook up without drying out. In this recipe, the starch in the pasta thickens up the sauce, making it even better.*

30 MINUTES OR LESS

Just Like Mom's Spaghetti 'n' Meatballs

Spend some time in any Italian neighborhood and, soon enough, your nose will lead you to the front door of someone's house, where mom's meatballs are simmering on the stove. Ya see, there's always at least one mom famous for making the best meatballs on the block, and everyone hopes she'll invite them over for dinner. Good thing you won't have to wait for your invitation, 'cause our recipe is just like Mom's!

Serves 2

Ingredients

¾ pound ground beef

⅓ cup plain bread crumbs

2 tablespoons grated Parmesan cheese

¼ cup water

1 tablespoon chopped fresh parsley

1 egg

1 teaspoon garlic powder

½ teaspoon salt

½ teaspoon black pepper

2 cups spaghetti sauce

½ pound spaghetti, prepared according to package directions

Preparation

1 Preheat oven to 350 degrees F. Coat a rimmed baking sheet with cooking spray.

2 In a large bowl, gently combine all ingredients except sauce and pasta; mix well. Form mixture into 6 meatballs and place on baking sheet. Bake 20 to 25 minutes, or until no longer pink in center.

3 In a saucepan over medium heat, heat sauce until hot. Add meatballs and simmer 5 minutes. Serve over hot pasta.

Test Kitchen Tip: *The key to plump and tender meatballs is not to over-mix, over-handle, or over-pack the meat mixture. Treat the ground beef with a little TLC and you'll end up with some of the best meatballs you've ever had.*

30 MINUTES OR LESS

Mexican Pasta Bake

We're always looking to our viewers and fans for new recipe ideas, so when we asked whether you all preferred Italian food vs. Mexican food and got a pretty divided response, we knew what had to be done: a culinary mash-up. Now, you can enjoy the best of both worlds in just one dish. Featuring both Italian and Mexican ingredients, this bake will please everyone.

Serves 2

Ingredients

2 cups penne pasta

½ pound ground beef

¼ cup chopped onion

1 cup spaghetti sauce

½ cup salsa

½ teaspoon ground cumin

½ teaspoon salt

1 cup ricotta cheese

1 cup shredded Mexican cheese blend, divided

1 tablespoon chopped fresh cilantro

Preparation

1 Preheat oven to 350 degrees F. Coat a 1-½-quart baking dish with cooking spray.

2 Prepare pasta according to package directions. Drain, rinse, and drain again; set aside in a medium bowl.

3 Meanwhile, in a large skillet over medium heat, cook ground beef and onion about 5 minutes, or until browned. Drain off excess liquid. Add to pasta along with spaghetti sauce, salsa, cumin, salt, ricotta cheese, ½ cup shredded cheese, and cilantro; stir until well combined. Spoon into baking dish.

4 Bake 25 minutes. Remove from oven and sprinkle with remaining ½ cup cheese. Return to oven and bake 5 more minutes, or until cheese is melted.

Great Go-Alongs

Nutty Garlic Green Beans

Here's proof that some of the simplest dishes are often some of the most loved. When we set out a variety of green bean dishes for our staff to taste and give feedback on, it was clear that this recipe was the winner by how fast they cleared the plate. It was so popular, that everyone wanted the recipe right then and there. Now, we're sharing this 5-ingredient recipe with you, so you can enjoy 'em whenever you want, too.

Serves 2

Ingredients

½ pound fresh green beans, trimmed

2 tablespoons olive oil

2 cloves garlic, thinly sliced

2 tablespoons chopped walnuts

¼ teaspoon salt

Preparation

1 In a saucepan over high heat, place beans and add enough water to cover. Bring to a boil and cook 6 to 8 minutes, or until tender; drain well. (Here is where you can customize these by cooking them a bit more or less depending on how you like your beans.)

2 In a skillet over medium heat, heat oil until hot. Add garlic, walnuts, and salt, and sauté until garlic starts to brown, stirring occasionally. Add green beans to garlic mixture, toss until evenly coated, and serve.

So Many Options: If you have a bag of frozen green beans, you can always use them in place of the fresh ones. If you do, rather than cooking them as suggested in step 1, simply microwave them until hot, and proceed as directed.

30 MINUTES OR LESS

Speedy Zucchini Fritters

If you find that your side dishes have been limited to simply microwaving whatever frozen veggies you have on hand, just because it's easy, then it's time to break that routine. Change things up by making these throw-together fritters that are ready in less time than it takes to go through your mail. Honestly, it's that easy.

Serves 2

Ingredients

2 cups grated zucchini (about 1 zucchini)

1 cup shredded cheddar cheese

½ cup all-purpose flour

½ teaspoon onion powder

½ teaspoon salt

¼ teaspoon black pepper

1 egg, lightly beaten

2 tablespoons vegetable oil

Preparation

1 In a large bowl, combine all ingredients except oil; mix well.

2 In a large skillet over medium heat, heat oil until hot. Drop heaping tablespoons of batter into skillet; be sure not to overcrowd. Cook 2 to 3 minutes per side, or until golden.

3 Remove to a paper towel-lined platter; repeat with remaining batter. Serve immediately.

Test Kitchen Tip: *There's no need to take out your food processor to grate the zucchini; a basic hand grater will do the trick in seconds. And if you like your fritters extra-crispy, then feel free to double the amount of oil.*

30 MINUTES OR LESS

Spaghetti Squash Italiano

We love spaghetti; we really do, but sometimes all those carbs can leave us feeling a bit sleepy. As much as we wish every mealtime was followed by naptime, that's not really the case. That's why we like to mix it up by making spaghetti squash from time to time. Spaghetti squash is such a fun veggie to eat, 'cause it not only shreds up to look like real noodles, but it's got a mild taste that takes on whatever flavors you make it with!

Serves 2

Ingredients

1 small spaghetti squash, cut in half lengthwise, and seeds removed

2 tablespoons olive oil

1 teaspoon garlic powder

½ teaspoon salt

¼ teaspoon black pepper

1 plum tomato, seeded and finely chopped

¼ cup shredded mozzarella cheese

1 tablespoon chopped fresh basil

Preparation

1 Preheat oven to 400 degrees F. Line a baking sheet with aluminum foil (for easy clean-up) and coat with cooking spray.

2 Drizzle each half of squash with oil, then sprinkle with garlic powder, salt, and pepper. Place squash cut-side down on baking sheet.

3 Bake 30 to 35 minutes, or until tender. Scrape inside of squash with a fork, shredding it into spaghetti-like strands. Leave shell intact.

4 Evenly divide tomatoes into each squash half; gently mix with squash. Top with mozzarella cheese. Place under broiler 3 to 5 minutes, or until cheese is melted. Sprinkle with basil and serve.

Test Kitchen Tip: *If you can't find a small squash, ask someone in the produce department if they would cut a larger one in half for you. That way the two of you can share a half.*

Lemon-Kissed "Burnt" Broccoli

Yes, we burned the broccoli, and no, we didn't do it by mistake. We found that when you roast certain vegetables until they're a little "burnt," it helps bring out their flavors even more. Add a drizzle of lemon juice and a sprinkle of cheese and you've turned an ordinary side dish into an extraordinary one. Just be warned, although this recipe is for two, it's easy to eat a double-portion by yourself.

Serves 2

Ingredients

1 tablespoon olive oil

¼ teaspoon salt

¼ teaspoon black pepper

3 cups broccoli florets

2 cloves garlic minced

1 teaspoon lemon juice

1 tablespoon grated Parmesan cheese

Preparation

1 Preheat oven to 400 degrees F.

2 In a bowl, combine oil, salt, and pepper. Add broccoli and garlic; toss until evenly coated. Place on a rimmed baking sheet.

3 Roast 20 to 25 minutes, or until the edges of the florets begin to char, turning over the broccoli halfway through the roasting. You can leave these in the oven a bit longer or shorter depending on how "burnt" you like these.

4 Drizzle lemon juice over broccoli, sprinkle with cheese, and serve.

Test Kitchen Tip: *Have a fresh lemon on hand? Cut it in half, then cut one of the halves into wedges to roast alongside the broccoli. When the broccoli's done, give the other half a squeeze over the broccoli. Talk about a double dose of lemony freshness!*

30 MINUTES OR LESS

Roasted Creamy Rosemary Onions

In the Test Kitchen we've had the chance to develop recipes for clients all over the country, including an onion grower from upstate New York. For this client, we roasted whole onions with fresh herbs and some simple seasonings. As soon as they came out of the oven, we knew we were onto something. Ya see, roasting 'em brings out their natural sweetness and makes 'em extra-tender and delicious. You may shed tears over this recipe, but they'll be tears of joy.

Serves 2

Ingredients

1 large onion, peeled, ends trimmed, and cut in half horizontally

¾ cup chicken broth

1 tablespoon olive oil

½ teaspoon chopped fresh rosemary

⅛ teaspoon salt

⅛ teaspoon black pepper

¼ cup heavy cream

2 teaspoons all-purpose flour

Ground nutmeg for sprinkling

Preparation

1 Preheat oven to 425 degrees F.

2 Place onion cut side up in a 1-quart baking dish. Pour chicken broth over onion and drizzle with olive oil. Sprinkle with rosemary, salt, and pepper. Bake uncovered 55 minutes, basting often.

3 In a small bowl, combine heavy cream and flour; whisk until smooth. Pour mixture over onion and sprinkle with nutmeg.

4 Bake 15 minutes, or until pan juices are thickened and onion is golden.

Test Kitchen Tips: *When we say a large onion, we mean large; not the biggest one in the small bag of onions, but the ones you buy by the pound. And yes, you can use any of the sweet varieties, like Vidalia or Texas sweet onions, or a white onion. Oh, and by the way, if you don't have fresh rosemary on hand, you can use ⅛ teaspoon of ground dried.*

Personal-Sized Spinach Soufflés

If Popeye could've tasted this spinach soufflé, he might have asked Olive Oyl to make this for dinner every single night. Just one bite of this dish can turn any spinach lover into a spinach enthusiast (or any non-spinach lover into a spinach believer). What makes these unique is how creamy and cheesy they are, with just the right combination of seasonings. Bake these tonight to experience a whole new level of yum!

Serves 2

Ingredients

½ cup heavy cream

1 egg

1 tablespoon grated Parmesan cheese

1 tablespoon all-purpose flour

½ teaspoon onion powder

½ teaspoon baking powder

1/8 teaspoon ground nutmeg

1/8 teaspoon salt

1/8 teaspoon black pepper

1 (10-ounce) package frozen chopped spinach, thawed and squeezed dry

Preparation

1 Preheat oven to 375 degrees F. Coat 2 (1-cup) ramekins with cooking spray.

2 In a bowl, whisk all ingredients, except spinach, until smooth. Add spinach; mix well and pour into ramekins.

3 Bake 20 to 25 minutes, or until a knife inserted in center comes out clean. Serve right out of the ramekins and enjoy.

Test Kitchen Tip: *The quickest way to thaw spinach is to put it in a bowl and microwave it until it comes apart easily. We recommend microwaving a minute or so at a time, making sure not to overheat it. Then, to get rid of all the water, drain it in a colander and squeeze it dry with your hands.*

30 MINUTES OR LESS

Honey Butter Roasted Carrots

Carrots are one of the sweeter veggies, which is why most people seem to like them as is. But if you really want to take these up a notch, then we suggest roasting them with our homemade honey butter glaze. It adds an extra bit of sticky sweetness that really enhances the flavor of the carrots. The two of you won't be able to get enough of 'em.

Serves 2

Ingredients

4 large carrots, peeled

1 tablespoon honey

1 tablespoon butter, melted

¼ teaspoon salt

⅛ teaspoon ground cinnamon

Preparation

1 Preheat oven to 425 degrees F. Line a baking sheet with aluminum foil (See Tip.) and coat with cooking spray.

2 Cut carrots in half and cut each half in quarters lengthwise.

3 In a medium bowl, whisk together honey, butter, salt, and cinnamon. Add carrots to mixture and toss until evenly coated. Place carrots on baking sheet lined with aluminum foil.

4 Bake 20 to 25 minutes on the top rack of your oven, or until carrots are tender and the edges begin to caramelize.

Note: If you like these a bit more "charred," finish 'em off under the broiler for just a minute or so. Be sure to keep an eye on them though!

Test Kitchen Tip: *We lined the pan with foil to make clean up a breeze, 'cause no one wants to spend all night scrubbing pots and pans!*

Veggie-Stuffed Zucchini Boats

In the summer, when our supermarkets and gardens are bursting with ripe red tomatoes and fresh zucchini, we love to make these stuffed zucchini boats. They're fresh-tasting, simple, and a great change of pace from all the other side dishes we enjoy throughout the rest of the year. In short, you'll both enjoy boatloads of yum!

Serves 2

Ingredients

1 medium zucchini, sliced in half lengthwise

1 tablespoon olive oil

2 tablespoons finely chopped onion

1 plum tomato, diced

2 tablespoons Italian-flavored bread crumbs

1 tablespoon grated Parmesan cheese

½ teaspoon garlic powder

¼ teaspoon salt

⅛ teaspoon black pepper

2 tablespoons shredded mozzarella cheese

Preparation

1 Preheat oven to 375 degrees F. Coat an 8-inch-square baking dish with cooking spray.

2 With a spoon, scoop meat out of zucchini halves, leaving a ¼-inch wall all around; set aside shells and finely chop the scooped-out zucchini meat.

3 In a medium skillet over medium heat, heat oil until hot. Sauté chopped zucchini, onion, and tomato 3 to 4 minutes, or until tender. Stir in bread crumbs, Parmesan cheese, garlic powder, salt, and pepper until well mixed. Spoon mixture evenly into zucchini shells and place in baking dish.

4 Cover tightly with aluminum foil and bake 25 to 30 minutes, or until zucchini shells are tender. Remove foil and sprinkle with mozzarella cheese. Bake 5 to 8 more minutes, or until cheese is melted.

Southern-Style Corn Pudding

We can't say for sure who's to thank for the original corn pudding recipe, but we do know that it's really popular in the South. Don't believe us? Just ask any Southern cook what side dish disappears quicker than any other on their table. Yup, it's the corn pudding. So, gather up your appetite, 'cause y'all are going to love our version of this Southern favorite made just for two.

Makes 2 very generous portions

Ingredients

1 (15-¼-ounce) can whole kernel corn, drained

1 (14-¾-ounce) can cream-style corn

2 tablespoons sugar

1 egg, beaten

1 tablespoon cornstarch

½ cup coarsely crushed butter crackers

1 tablespoon butter, melted

Preparation

1 Preheat oven to 375 degrees F. Coat a 1-quart baking dish with cooking spray.

2 In a large bowl, combine kernel corn, cream-style corn, sugar, egg, and cornstarch; mix well. Spoon into baking dish.

3 In a small bowl, combine crackers and butter. Mix well and sprinkle on top of corn mixture.

4 Bake 30 to 35 minutes, or until golden and set.

Decisions, Decisions: At this point in the book, you've either dug out your ramekins or have already picked up a set to have on hand. In any case, if you'd like to bake this dish in individual portions, go for it. Just remember, the cooking time will be about 25% quicker, so keep an eye on them. And, since ramekins vary in size, you may need to make a third one (but who's complaining?).

Bubblin' Bacon Bean Bake

Baked beans are often cooked in large batches for summer barbecues, but that doesn't mean you have to wait until ya see the firework tents to make 'em, or that baked beans must always make enough to feed a crowd. With our recipe, you'll end up with sweet and tangy baked beans that are big on taste, but not so big that they can feed all your relatives, your neighbors, your friends, your neighbors' friends...you get the idea.

Serves 2

Ingredients

1 (16-ounce) can baked beans

1 tablespoon minced onion

2 tablespoons molasses

1 tablespoon yellow mustard

2 slices bacon, cut in half

2 teaspoons light brown sugar

Preparation

1 Preheat oven to 350 degrees F. Coat a 1-quart baking dish with cooking spray.

2 In a bowl, combine beans, onion, molasses, and mustard; mix well then pour into baking dish.

3 Top with bacon and sprinkle with brown sugar. Bake 25 to 30 minutes, or until bubbly and the bacon is cooked. Serve immediately.

__Did You Know?__ Starting with canned baked beans saves a whole lot of time. Just think, while some folks are baking their beans for hours, you're getting the same flavors you love by adding your own seasonings to pre-baked beans.

30 MINUTES OR LESS

Roasted Salt & Pepper Red Potatoes

There's something about small food that brings out the kid in all of us. We love mini pastries, bite-sized hors d'oeuvres, and even "fun-sized" candy bars. So, we're willing to bet you're going to love these small roasted potatoes, too. Not only are they as cute as a button, but their crispy seasoned coating makes them so yummy. Plus, since they're small, they cook up in about half the time of traditional baked potatoes. Hooray for tiny 'taters!

Serves 2

Ingredients

1 pound
red creamer potatoes

1 tablespoon olive oil

1 teaspoon kosher salt

¼ teaspoon coarsely ground
black pepper

Preparation

1 Preheat oven to 400 degrees F.

2 Place potatoes in a bowl and toss with olive oil until evenly coated. Sprinkle with salt and pepper on all sides. Place on a baking sheet.

3 Bake 30 to 35 minutes, or until fork-tender and crispy on the outside.

Note: Not familiar with creamer potatoes? They're simply small red or yellow potatoes, sometimes called salt, new, or baby potatoes.

Test Kitchen Tip: *We recommend using kosher or sea salt and coarsely ground black pepper in this recipe, since they'll work together to create a really crispy coating. While regular table grind salt and pepper will work, we like the crunch that comes with using the bigger grind.*

30 MINUTES OR LESS

Greek Smashed Potatoes

There are endless ways to make potatoes. You can mash 'em, bake 'em, fry 'em, boil 'em...or hey, you can even combine a couple of ways in one! To make these, we boil, then smash them, before seasoning them with a lemony Greek dressing. You could say we got the idea from the traditional plate smashing that goes on at Greek weddings, but really we were looking for a tasty-fun way for the two of you to get "smashed" together.

Serves 2

Ingredients

1 pound small white potatoes

2 tablespoon olive oil

1 teaspoon lemon juice

½ teaspoon oregano

½ teaspoon salt

¼ teaspoon black pepper

Preparation

1 In a large saucepan over high heat, place potatoes and cover with water; bring to a boil. Once boiling, reduce heat to medium and simmer about 25 minutes, or until potatoes are just tender; drain and let cool slightly.

2 Preheat oven to 450 degrees F. Coat a baking sheet with cooking spray. Place potatoes on baking sheet. Using a large spoon, or the heel of your hand, gently press down on each potato to smash it so it ends up about ½-inch thick. Make sure you keep the potato as one piece.

3 In a small bowl, combine oil, lemon juice, oregano, salt, and pepper; mix well. Brush half the mixture on top of potatoes.

4 Bake 15 minutes, or until bottoms begin to brown. Flip the potatoes and brush with remaining oil mixture. Bake an additional 12 to 15 minutes, or until both sides are browned and crispy. Serve piping hot.

Barbecue Potato Tots

You know what goes well with a Friday night TV marathon? Tots. We're not talking plain ol' tots either. We're talking potato tots that are smothered in BBQ sauce, lots of Cheddar, and sliced jalapeños. The kind of tots you don't mind skipping pizza for. Just thinking of all that cheesy goodness makes our mouths start to water.

Serves 2

Ingredients

2 cups frozen potato tots

¼ cup barbecue sauce

¼ cup shredded cheddar cheese

1 tablespoon sliced pickled jalapeños

Preparation

1 Preheat oven to 325 degrees F. Line a rimmed baking sheet with aluminum foil and coat foil with cooking spray. Place potatoes on baking sheet.

2 Bake 15 to 20 minutes, or until crispy. Remove from oven, drizzle with barbecue sauce, and sprinkle with cheese and jalapeño slices.

3 Bake 5 minutes more, or until cheese is melted, and serve immediately.

So Many Options: Make "Tots 'n' TV" a tradition by mixing up the toppings every week! Another one of our favorites is the cheeseburger version. To make it this way, just swap out the barbecue sauce for ketchup, and top with pickle slices instead of jalapeños. What other tasty ideas can the two of you come up with?

30 MINUTES OR LESS

Cinnamon-Pecan Spiral Sweet Potatoes

We can think of a few reasons why you would want to make this recipe. First, and most importantly, these sweet potatoes taste crazy good. You just can't put into words what the cinnamon, sugar, and pecans add to this recipe. Second, they look impressive (hint, hint...great for date night!). Third, they're easy to make and they cook up in no time (yup, a weeknight favorite!). Should we go on, or is the oven already preheating?

Serves 2

Ingredients

½ cup chopped pecans

1 tablespoon light brown sugar

¼ teaspoon ground cinnamon

⅛ teaspoon salt

1 tablespoon butter, softened

2 large sweet potatoes, scrubbed well

1 tablespoon vegetable oil

Preparation

1 Preheat oven to 400 degrees F. In a small bowl, combine pecans, brown sugar, cinnamon, salt, and butter. Mix until crumbly and set aside.

2 On a cutting board, place 2 wooden spoons parallel to one another and place a potato lengthwise between the handles. Make 8 crosswise cuts, about ¾ of the way through the potato, stopping each time the knife hits the handle of the wooden spoons. Repeat with remaining potato.

3 Rub the oil evenly over the potatoes. Place them on a baking sheet and bake 55 to 60 minutes, or until tender. Evenly divide the pecan mixture between the slits of the potatoes and over the top.

4 Bake an additional 5 to 8 minutes, or until brown sugar and butter topping begins to caramelize.

Finishing Touch: *If you want to add even more sweetness to your potatoes, you could always drizzle on a bit of maple syrup or honey right before serving. Just make sure it's only a little 'cause a little goes a long way!*

California Quinoa Salad

Okay, let's get this out of the way; it's pronounced KEEN-wah, and it's one of the trendiest side dishes of the decade. The way we make it is so fresh-tasting and colorful, it's guaranteed to brighten up any meal. And 'cause it's loaded with fresh fruit and veggies, it's perfect for those days when you're looking to eat healthier. Pair it with a piece of lean chicken or fish for a complete nutritious meal.

Serves 2

Ingredients

½ cup quinoa

½ cup diced mango

⅓ cup shelled frozen edamame, thawed

¼ cup diced red bell pepper

1 tablespoon chopped red onion

1 tablespoon sliced almonds

2 tablespoons rice wine vinegar

½ teaspoon lime zest

¼ teaspoon salt

Preparation

1 Cook quinoa according to package directions; let cool.

2 In a bowl, combine cooked quinoa, mango, edamame, bell pepper, red onion, and almonds. Add vinegar, lime zest, and salt, and toss until evenly coated. Serve, or refrigerate until ready to serve.

Test Kitchen Tip: *To make sure the quinoa doesn't have a bitter taste, rinse it well before cooking it. Simply place it in a fine mesh strainer and run cold water over it for a minute or so.*

30 MINUTES OR LESS

Mushroom Risotto

For years, home cooks have avoided making risotto 'cause they weren't quite sure if it was something they could easily make at home. The truth is, this rice dish has a fancy Italian name and a fancy Italian taste, but it's really quite simple. Our three-step method is so easy, you'll have time to sauté chicken breasts and throw together a salad, too. The end result? You'll have a wow-worthy dish ready in just 20 minutes

Serves 2

Ingredients

2 cups chicken broth

2 tablespoons butter, divided

1 cup sliced fresh mushrooms

¼ cup finely chopped onion

¾ cup uncooked Arborio rice

1 teaspoon minced garlic

1 tablespoon grated Parmesan cheese

1 teaspoon chopped fresh parsley

⅛ teaspoon black pepper

Preparation

1 In a saucepan over medium heat, bring chicken broth to a simmer, but do not boil. Reduce heat to low and keep warm.

2 Meanwhile, in another saucepan over medium-high heat, melt 1 tablespoon butter. Add mushrooms and onions and sauté 4 to 5 minutes, or until softened. Stir in rice, and garlic. Add ½ cup of hot broth to rice and stir constantly until broth is absorbed. Add remaining broth ½ cup at a time, stirring constantly until each addition of broth is absorbed before adding the next. (This takes about 15 minutes total.)

3 Remove from heat. Stir in remaining 1 tablespoon butter, the cheese, parsley, and pepper. Serve immediately.

Did You Know? *Arborio rice is a short-grain rice that has a creamy consistency when cooked, which makes it the perfect rice for dishes like risotto and rice pudding. It's available in practically every supermarket, right alongside all the other rice varieties.*

30 MINUTES OR LESS

Delectable Desserts

Caramel German Chocolate Cupcakes

German chocolate cake originated in America. Yep, the "German" in its name actually comes from the chocolate maker who first developed the type of chocolate used to make this cake. Interesting, huh? It's almost as interesting as taking your first bite into this decadent, caramel-drizzled cupcake. Actually, nevermind...digging into this cupcake is much, much better.

Makes 2

Ingredients

¼ cup all-purpose flour

2 tablespoons sugar

1 tablespoon cocoa powder

¼ teaspoon baking soda

⅛ teaspoon salt

2 tablespoons vegetable oil

2 tablespoons milk

¼ teaspoon vanilla extract

Chocolate frosting (see Note)

1 tablespoon chopped pecans

1 tablespoon shredded coconut

Caramel sauce for drizzling

Preparation

1 Preheat oven to 325 degrees F. Place 2 cupcake liners in a muffin tin.

2 In a small bowl, combine flour, sugar, cocoa powder, baking soda, and salt. Add oil, milk, and vanilla; mix well. Pour batter evenly into cupcake liners.

3 Bake 18 to 20 minutes, or until top of cupcakes are firm. [See Tip.] Let cool.

4 Frost cupcakes with chocolate frosting, then sprinkle with pecans and coconut. Drizzle caramel sauce over the top.

Note: The recipe for Fudgy Chocolate Frosting can be found on page 228, or use your favorite canned chocolate frosting.

Test Kitchen Tip: *We don't recommend using the toothpick test to check for doneness with these, as we discovered it causes the cupcakes to fall in the center.*

Key Lime Cupcakes

Take a stroll down Duval Street in Key West, Florida, and you're bound to come across some of the best places for Key lime pie in the whole country. After tasting some of the local varieties, we were inspired to make a version of this dessert in cupcake form – that way you two can enjoy it wherever ya want, whether on the beach, at the pool, or in the comfort of your own cozy kitchen.

Makes 2

Ingredients

1 egg white

2 tablespoons sugar

2 tablespoons butter, melted

½ teaspoon vanilla extract

1 tablespoon Key lime juice (see Note)

¼ cup all-purpose flour

¼ teaspoon baking powder

⅛ teaspoon salt

1 teaspoon milk

Vanilla frosting (see Finishing Touch)

Lime zest for garnish

Preparation

1 Preheat oven to 350 degrees F. Place 2 cupcake liners in a muffin tin.

2 In a small bowl, whisk egg white and sugar until frothy. Stir in butter, vanilla, and lime juice. Add flour, baking powder, salt, and milk, and gently stir until smooth. Pour batter evenly into cupcake liners.

3 Bake 13 to 15 minutes, or until toothpick comes out dry. Let cool.

4 Frost cupcakes with vanilla frosting. Garnish with lime zest.

Note: Can't find Key lime juice? No problem, regular lime juice will work just fine.

Finishing Touch: *The recipe for our homemade Very Vanilla Frosting, which makes just enough for two cupcakes, can be found on page 228. To give these cupcakes plenty of pucker-up flavor, we suggest you substitute 2 teaspoons of Key lime juice for the milk in the recipe. Or, if you'd rather, you can use a ½ cup of store-bought vanilla frosting and stir in a few drops of Key lime juice, until the frosting has just the right touch of lime flavor.*

Fudgy Chocolate Frosting

Let's set the scene: Mom is whipping up her homemade fudgy chocolate frosting and you're standing next to her. Are you: A) waiting till she turns around to dip your finger in for a taste, or B) begging Mom to let you "clean" the bowl when she's done? Good thing you no longer have to make such hard decisions!

Makes enough for 2 cupcakes

Ingredients

2 tablespoons butter, softened

¼ teaspoon vanilla extract

1 tablespoon cocoa powder

½ cup confectioners' sugar

2 teaspoons milk

Preparation

1 In a small bowl, whisk butter, vanilla, and cocoa powder until thoroughly blended. Add confectioners' sugar and milk and mix until smooth. Use immediately, or refrigerate until ready to use.

Very Vanilla Frosting

It's hard to believe that in a world with so many flavors, vanilla is still the most popular choice. We think it means that the world has a true appreciation for great-tasting classics. This frosting is great on top of our cupcakes, but we won't deny that we think it's great right off the spoon, too!

Makes enough for 2 cupcakes

Ingredients

2 tablespoons butter, softened

½ cup plus 2 tablespoons confectioners' sugar

¼ teaspoon vanilla extract

2 teaspoons milk

Preparation

1 In a small bowl, whisk butter, confectioners' sugar, vanilla, and milk until smooth. Use immediately or refrigerate until ready to use.

30 MINUTES OR LESS

Can-Do Carrot Cake

You love cake, but you find that you can't make it all that often 'cause it's just the two of you and you'll both end up eating way more than ya want to, or it'll go stale before you come close to finishing it. Not anymore! With our recipe, you can turn your can't-do into a CAN-do, 'cause we've come up with a delicious batter that bakes up perfectly every time, and cooks up in a pretty unexpected way...

Serves 2

Ingredients

½ cup sugar

½ cup all-purpose flour

½ teaspoon baking soda

¼ teaspoon ground cinnamon

¼ teaspoon salt

1 egg

2 tablespoons vegetable oil

½ cup grated carrots

¼ cup flaked coconut

2 tablespoons chopped walnuts

1 cup cream cheese frosting (from a 16-ounce can)

Preparation

1 Preheat oven to 350 degrees F. Coat 2 (12-ounce) empty and cleaned tuna cans (yes, tuna cans!) with cooking spray.

2 In a large bowl, combine all ingredients except frosting; beat with an electric mixer until batter is smooth. Pour evenly into tuna cans.

3 Bake 25 to 30 minutes, or until a toothpick inserted in center comes out clean. Let cool 15 minutes, then remove from cans gently and place on wire rack to finish cooling.

4 Place one cake layer on a plate and frost top of layer. Place second layer on top and frost top and sides of cake.

Note: No tuna cans, no problem. You could bake this in 2 small baking dishes (about 12-ounces each).

Finishing Touch: When stacking the cakes, you may want to trim off the domed part, so the layers stack nice and level. And after you're done frosting it, crumble those trimmings and use 'em to decorate the bottom edge of the cake.

Old-Fashioned Strawberry Patch Shortcakes

This dessert has summer written all over it, 'cause it's the kind that makes ya want to throw on some overalls and head out to a strawberry patch, so you can choose the ripest and juiciest strawberries to make it with. To go along with that old-fashioned country feel, this dessert is assembled inside two Mason jars—one for you, and one for whomever you like best. Maybe they can be in charge of the lemonade?

Makes 2

Ingredients

1 cup heavy cream

½ teaspoon vanilla extract

3 tablespoons confectioners' sugar

2 slices pound cake, cut into ½-inch cubes (see Tip)

1 cup sliced strawberries

Preparation

1 In a medium bowl, combine heavy cream and vanilla; beat with an electric mixer 1 minute. Slowly add sugar and continue beating until stiff peaks form; set aside.

2 In each of 2 [8- to 10-ounce] Mason jars, layer ¼ of the pound cake, ¼ of the strawberries, and ¼ of the whipped cream. Repeat layers 1 more time. Serve immediately.

Test Kitchen Tip: *You've got a couple of options when it comes to the pound cake. You can either pick up a couple of slices of individually wrapped pound cake, which can typically be found in the bakery or near the checkout line of your grocery store, or you can buy a frozen pound cake, cut some slices, and freeze the rest for another time.*

30 MINUTES OR LESS

Summer's Best Lemon Pudding Cakes

We've all heard the expression, "when life gives you lemons, make lemonade." Well, that's a good idea, but we think we've come up with a better one, "when life gives you lemons, make lemon pudding cakes." Ya see, this light-as-can-be dessert is packed with so much lemony deliciousness it's guaranteed to brighten your day, and theirs too!

Makes 2

Ingredients

1 egg, separated

⅓ cup buttermilk

1 tablespoon lemon juice

1 teaspoon lemon zest

¼ cup sugar

2 tablespoons all-purpose flour

⅛ teaspoon salt

Fresh fruit for garnish (optional)

Preparation

1 Preheat oven to 325 degrees F. Coat 2 (1-cup) ramekins with cooking spray.

2 In a small bowl, with an electric mixer, beat egg white until stiff peaks form. Set aside.

3 In a medium bowl beat egg yolk, buttermilk, lemon juice, and lemon zest until thoroughly combined. Using a rubber spatula, fold in the sugar, flour, and salt. Gently fold the egg white into the egg yolk mixture a little at a time.

4 Divide batter evenly between the ramekins. Place ramekins in an 8-inch square baking dish and fill with water until halfway up sides of ramekins.

5 Bake 25 to 30 minutes, or until tops of cakes spring back when lightly pressed. Remove ramekins from water bath and cool on a wire rack 5 to 10 minutes. Carefully invert cakes onto serving plates. Serve immediately or let cool completely, then refrigerate and serve chilled. Before serving, feel free to garnish with fresh fruit, if desired.

Pineapple Upside-Down Cake Parfaits

If life has the two of you feeling a bit upside-down lately, then we've got an idea for the perfect staycation that'll cheer ya both right up. All you've gotta do is turn on some island music, dig out your flowered leis and grass skirts, and make these tropical pineapple parfaits. We guarantee that the combination of silliness and yumminess will leave you feeling right-side up again.

Makes 2

Ingredients

1 (8-ounce) can pineapple slices, drained, with 1 tablespoon juice reserved

2 tablespoons butter

½ cup light brown sugar

½ teaspoon vanilla extract

3 slices pound cake, cut into 1-inch cubes (see Tip)

Whipped cream for topping

2 maraschino cherries

Preparation

1 Cut pineapple slices in half. In a medium skillet over medium heat, melt butter and brown sugar, stirring occasionally. Add vanilla, pineapple slices, and reserved pineapple juice, and cook 1 to 2 minutes, or until warm.

2 Place the cake cubes into 2 parfait or wine glasses, dividing evenly. Spoon the brown sugar sauce over the cake cubes and top with pineapple slices.

3 Top each parfait with whipped cream and a cherry. Serve immediately.

Note: For even more of a tropical taste, go ahead and replace the reserved pineapple juice with a tablespoon or two of your favorite island rum.

Test Kitchen Tip: *We used a frozen pound cake and cut the slices while it was still frozen. Then, we put the rest back into the freezer. If you do this, then you'll have pound cake on hand the next time ya want to make this, or you can use it when ya want to whip up our Old-Fashioned Strawberry Patch Shortcakes (page 232).*

30 MINUTES OR LESS

Black & White Cookie Cheesecakes

These New York-style cheesecakes may be small in size, but don't let that fool ya, they're big on taste. They're decadently rich, just like you would find in some of the most famous New York delis, but they've got something extra-special going on...a chocolate cookie crust. It's the ultimate for anyone who likes cheesecake.

Makes 2

Ingredients

⅓ cup finely crushed mini chocolate sandwich cookies

1 tablespoon butter, melted

6 ounces cream cheese, softened

¼ cup sugar

1 egg

¼ teaspoon vanilla extract

Whipped cream for garnish

Mini chocolate sandwich cookies for garnish

Preparation

1 Preheat oven to 350 degrees F. Coat 2 (1-cup) ramekins with cooking spray and place on a baking sheet.

2 In a small bowl, mix together cookie crumbs and butter. Press into bottom of each ramekin.

3 In a medium bowl, beat cream cheese and sugar until smooth. Add egg and vanilla and beat until creamy. Divide batter evenly between ramekins.

4 Bake 18 to 20 minutes, or until tops are firm. (The cheesecakes may still jiggle slightly when removing from oven.) Let cool to room temperature, then refrigerate at least 4 hours, or until ready to serve. Garnish with whipped cream and mini chocolate sandwich cookies.

Test Kitchen Tip: *If you're like us in the Test Kitchen, then we suggest that you buy a snack-sized bag of mini chocolate sandwich cookies rather than the big bag. The reason is, if we buy the big bag, we'll end up eating the big bag...if ya know what we mean!*

Peach Melba Rustic Pies

If you've got peaches and you've got raspberries, then you've got the makings of a Peach Melba. And we've found that one of the tastiest ways to enjoy this fruity combo is baked into a pie (make that two pies!). Rustic in taste and look, these pies have a real down-home feeling to 'em that's even better when they're served warm. Heck, ya might even want to go the extra mile and top 'em with a scoop of vanilla ice cream. Now that's good!

Makes 2

Ingredients

1 refrigerated pie crust (from a 14.1-ounce package), cut in half

3 cups frozen and thawed sliced peaches

½ cup fresh raspberries

1 tablespoon sugar

1 tablespoon peach jelly

Confectioners' sugar for sprinkling

Preparation

1 Preheat oven to 425 degrees F. Place both halves of pie crust on a rimmed baking sheet.

2 In a large bowl, combine peaches, raspberries, and sugar; toss to coat. Arrange mixture in center of each dough piece, leaving a 1-inch border. Fold edges of dough over the edge of the fruit filling, toward center, overlapping slightly. (See photo.)

3 Place jelly in a small microwave-safe bowl and microwave until melted. Brush melted jelly over peach mixture and edges of dough.

4 Bake 10 minutes, then reduce oven temperature to 350 degrees. Bake 20 more minutes, or until lightly browned. Sprinkle with confectioners' sugar. Serve warm or at room temperature.

So Many Options: If fresh peaches are plentiful, go ahead and use 'em—just make sure ya peel them before cutting into slices! And when it comes to the jelly, feel free to swap with apple or apricot, if that's what you've got in the fridge.

Just-the-Right-Size Chocolate Cream Pies

If you've ever had to stop yourself from buying a pie at your favorite bakery, 'cause you didn't think the two of you could (or should) eat the whole thing on your own, then boy is this recipe going to be a real treat for both of you. These pies are just the right size for each of you to go to town on without feeling guilty.

Serves 2

Ingredients

1 refrigerated pie crust (from a 14.1-ounce package)

1 (3.25-ounce) store-bought chocolate pudding cup

Whipped cream for topping

1 chocolate candy bar

Preparation

1 Preheat oven to 450 degrees F.

2 Unroll pie crust onto a cutting board. Cut 6 (3-½-inch) circles out of dough. (See Note.) Place the dough into bottom and up sides of 6 muffin tin cups.

3 Bake 8 to 10 minutes, or until golden. Remove from tin and let cool. Fill 2 crusts with pudding. (Place the remaining 4 crusts in a plastic storage container and freeze for another time.)

4 Dollop each with whipped cream. Now for the fun part. Using a vegetable peeler, create chocolate curls by running the peeler blade over the edge of the chocolate bar, then garnish as shown.

Test Kitchen Tips:

• *If you don't have a 3-½-inch round cookie cutter, just grab a ruler and find a drinking glass, coffee mug, plastic storage container, or clean can that's about the right size. Then, place that on the dough and use it as a template to cut out each circle with a paring knife.*

• *The frozen crusts will last up to 2 months in the freezer. When you get a craving, simply take them out, fill 'em with your favorite pudding flavor, or even pie filling, and enjoy!*

30 MINUTES OR LESS

Bite-Sized Southern Pecan Tassies

If the only time you ever have pecan pie is around the holidays, then this recipe is going to change everything. You see, we took a tip from the South, where every day is a good day for pecan pie, and came up with this recipe for bite-sized pecan tassies that are as addictive as you're imagining right now. Now you can both give in to temptation by having just a few bites from your own small batch.

Makes 10

Ingredients

4 tablespoons (½ stick) butter, softened

2 ounces cream cheese, softened

½ cup all-purpose flour

1 egg

½ tablespoon butter, melted

¼ cup light brown sugar

⅛ teaspoon salt

¼ teaspoon vanilla extract

2 tablespoons coarsely chopped pecans

Preparation

1 In a large bowl with an electric mixer, beat together butter and cream cheese. Add flour and mix until well incorporated. (It might not come together into a dough just yet.) Using your hands, gently squeeze the mixture, creating a ball. Wrap with plastic wrap and chill 20 minutes.

2 Meanwhile, preheat oven to 350 degrees F. Coat 10 cups in a mini muffin tin with cooking spray. (Yes, mini.) Shape dough into 10 equal balls. Place each dough ball into a muffin cup. Using your thumb, press dough into each cup, forming a crust.

3 In a small bowl, whisk egg, melted butter, brown sugar, salt, vanilla, and pecans. Spoon mixture evenly into crusts.

4 Bake 15 to 20 minutes, or until the pecan filling is firm and crusts are golden. Cool slightly, then remove to a wire rack to cool completely.

Test Kitchen Tip: *After they've cooled, you might need to run a paring knife around the edge of each cup to help get them out of the pan.*

Grown-Up Mocha Milkshakes

This isn't the chocolate milkshake you begged Mom to make for you after school. This milkshake is all grown up, just like you, which means it's got a little more sophistication and a whole lot more edge.

Serves 2

Ingredients

4 large scoops coffee ice cream

2 tablespoons coffee-flavored liqueur (optional)

1 tablespoon cocoa powder

Pinch of ground cinnamon

²/₃ cup milk

Whipped cream for topping

Chocolate-flavored syrup for topping

Preparation

1 In a blender, combine ice cream, liqueur, if desired, cocoa powder, cinnamon, and milk; blend until smooth.

2 Pour into glasses, and top with whipped cream and chocolate syrup. Serve immediately.

Finishing Touch: *If you want to go all out, sprinkle on some extra cinnamon and a few chocolate-covered coffee beans.*

30 MINUTES OR LESS

Fresh-Picked Strawberry Milkshakes

In the summer, when strawberries are so abundant and so reasonably priced, this is the perfect go-to treat. And, unlike most ice cream parlor strawberry milkshakes that ya may have had in the past, this one is bursting with berry-liciousness since it's loaded with so many fresh strawberries.

Serves 2

Ingredients

¾ cup milk

1 pound strawberries (about 2 cups), hulled

3 large scoops vanilla ice cream

1 teaspoon vanilla extract

Whipped cream for topping

Preparation

1 In a blender, combine all ingredients, except whipped cream, and blend until smooth.

2 Pour into glasses, top with whipped cream, and serve immediately.

Did You Know? When fresh strawberries are plentiful, you can hull some extras and freeze them. That way, when they're not as readily available, you can still enjoy the fresh-picked taste that these milkshakes deliver.

30 MINUTES OR LESS

Deep Dish Hot Fudge Brownie Sundaes

We're giving the phrase "Sunday Funday" a whole new meaning with our chocolate brownie sundae that's guaranteed to make any day a "fun day." Just imagine the look on their face when you surprise them with their own freshly baked brownie sundae. And when you set out a few of their favorite toppings like nuts, whipped cream, and candy pieces, it'll be the cherry on top!

Makes 2

Ingredients

½ stick (4 tablespoons) butter

¾ cup plus 2 teaspoons semisweet chocolate chips, divided

1 egg

⅓ cup sugar

¼ cup all-purpose flour

½ teaspoon vanilla extract

⅛ teaspoon salt

2 scoops vanilla ice cream

Preparation

1 Preheat oven to 350 degrees F. Coat 2 (1-cup) ramekins with cooking spray.

2 In a microwave-safe bowl, combine butter and ¾ cup chocolate chips. Microwave 60 seconds, stir, and continue microwaving for 10-second intervals until chocolate is melted and smooth.

3 In a medium bowl, whisk egg and sugar. Whisk in melted chocolate until blended. Add flour, vanilla, and salt, and whisk until thoroughly combined. Divide batter evenly between ramekins. Divide remaining 2 teaspoons chocolate chips onto the middle of each; press lightly into batter.

4 Bake 18 to 20 minutes, or until top is firm and starts to crack. (The center will still be a bit gooey.) Let cool slightly, then top with ice cream and serve.

So Many Options: We used vanilla ice cream in our recipe, but if the thought of double chocolate makes your eyes light up, then go ahead and use chocolate ice cream instead, or use any other flavor you love!

Crispy-Coated Ice Cream Balls

Ever heard of fried ice cream? It's a thing, we promise! Actually, it's not unusual to find this deep-fried treat on a dessert menu at a Mexican restaurant, or even at the state fair. Well, this is our take on that dessert. Instead of getting messy with a fryer, we came up with an "oven-fried" way to give your favorite creamy ice cream a crispy and buttery coating that's simply to die for.

Makes 2

Ingredients

1 pint vanilla ice cream

1 cup frosted corn flake cereal, coarsely crushed

½ tablespoon butter, melted

¼ teaspoon ground cinnamon

2 tablespoons butterscotch ice cream topping

Preparation

1 Line an 8-inch square baking dish with wax paper. With a large ice cream scoop or spoon, form 2 ice cream balls, each about 2-½ inches in diameter. Place in baking dish, then freeze about 30 minutes, or until firm.

2 Meanwhile, preheat oven to 350 degrees F. Coat a rimmed baking sheet with cooking spray. In a small bowl, combine cereal, butter and cinnamon; mix well and spread on baking sheet. Bake 5 to 7 minutes, or until lightly browned and crisp. Let cool, then place in a shallow dish.

3 When ice cream is hard, roll in cereal mixture, coating on all sides and gently pressing coating onto each ball to coat well. Return to baking dish and freeze until ready to serve. Drizzle with butterscotch right before serving.

Super-Fun Shaved Watermelon Ice

This dessert is super-fun, super-refreshing, and super-easy, which makes it great for those hot summer days when all ya really want to do is kick back and relax with your favorite person next to you. We love how the mini chocolate chips make it look like we've sprinkled watermelon seeds on top!

Serves 2

Ingredients

2 tablespoons water

3 tablespoons sugar

2 teaspoons honey

2 teaspoons lemon juice

2 cups seedless watermelon chunks

1 teaspoon mini chocolate chips

Fresh mint for garnish (optional)

Preparation

1 In a small saucepan over high heat, bring water, sugar, and honey to a boil, stirring until sugar is dissolved. Remove syrup from heat and let cool. Stir in lemon juice.

2 In a blender, combine watermelon chunks and syrup; puree until smooth. Pour into a loaf pan. Cover and freeze 1 to 2 hours, or until frozen 1 inch around edges. (The edges will get a little icy.)

3 Stir well, then cover and freeze 2 to 3 additional hours, or until completely frozen. Using a fork, scrape ice until it's snow-like. When ready to serve, using an ice cream scoop, dish into bowls and top with chocolate chips. Garnish with fresh mint, if desired, and serve.

So Many Options: *There's more than one way to give this dessert its snow-like consistency. Instead of using a fork, like we mention above, you could freeze this in an ice cube tray. Once it's frozen, place the cubes into your food processor with a cutting blade, and pulse them until you get the desired consistency.*

Chocolate Almond Croissants

It's hard to put into words how good a buttery and flaky croissant, filled with a thick layer of rich chocolate and topped with sliced almonds is, so we just have to urge you to give it a try for yourself. If you do find a way to describe its perfection, please share your ideas on our Facebook page. We'd love to hear what you think of this delectable dessert.

Makes 2

Ingredients

1 cup chocolate chips

1 teaspoon butter

¼ teaspoon vanilla extract

2 regular-sized (not mini) croissants, cut in half horizontally

2 tablespoons sliced almonds

Preparation

1 In a small saucepan over low heat, combine chocolate chips and butter, and warm until melted, stirring constantly. Stir in vanilla.

2 Spread all but 1 tablespoon chocolate evenly on the cut side of the bottom of each croissant. Place the top of the croissant over the chocolate.

3 Drizzle each croissant with remaining chocolate (warming for a few seconds in the microwave, if necessary), and sprinkle with almonds. Let cool slightly until chocolate firms up, then serve.

Serving Suggestion: If you don't have the chance to eat these right away, you can pop them in the microwave about 10 to 15 seconds, which should be just long enough to soften up the chocolate and give the filling just the right consistency for creamy, chocolatey yummy.

30 MINUTES OR LESS

Fancy French Crème Brûlée

The best part of eating crème brûlée is using your spoon to crack the surface of the hard candied topping and digging into the creamy custard below. And while most French chefs believe the only way to get this topping is to use a pastry torch (a fancy name for a small blow torch), we knew there had to be a simpler way. Now, you can enjoy this restaurant-quality dessert whenever ya want, no fancy tools required.

Makes 2

Ingredients

1 cup heavy cream

¼ cup milk

½ cup sugar, divided

3 egg yolks

1 teaspoon vanilla extract

Preparation

1 In a medium saucepan over medium heat, combine heavy cream, milk, ¼ cup sugar, the egg yolks, and vanilla. Cook 15 minutes, stirring frequently. (Be careful not to boil.) Mixture will thicken slightly.

2 Remove from heat and with an electric mixer, beat 3 minutes, or until it becomes the consistency of thin pudding. Divide equally between 2 (1-cup) custard cups or ramekins. Chill 3 to 4 hours, or until custard sets.

3 In a small skillet over medium heat, melt remaining ¼ cup sugar until golden, then pour over chilled custards. Be careful as the sugar mixture will be very hot! Chill 15 to 20 additional minutes, or until sugar hardens. Serve immediately, or keep chilled until ready to serve. (See Test Kitchen Tip.)

Test Kitchen Tip: *These can be topped with melted sugar and chilled up to 2 hours before serving. So, if making these in advance, plan to top with sugar within 2 hours of serving.*

Fruit Crêpes with Chocolate Hazelnut Drizzle

This fancy schmancy dessert can double as a fancy schmancy breakfast, which basically means it's okay to have it anytime ya want. And while you can fill a crêpe with practically anything, we think there's nothing better than the classic combination of strawberries, bananas, and creamy rich chocolate hazelnut spread. Just wait till the two of you taste it!

Makes 2

Ingredients

2 ready-made crêpes (from a 5-ounce package) (see note)

2 tablespoons chocolate hazelnut spread, plus additional for drizzling (see Note)

1 cup sliced strawberries

2 bananas, sliced

Confectioners' sugar for sprinkling

Preparation

1 Place crêpes on a flat surface; spread evenly with chocolate hazelnut spread. Evenly arrange strawberries and bananas down center of crêpes.

2 Fold one side of each crepe over the fruit, then fold over the other side. Sprinkle with confectioners' sugar, drizzle with hazelnut spread, and serve.

Note: If the chocolate hazelnut spread is too thick to drizzle, warm it in the microwave for just a few seconds.

Did You Know? You can find refrigerated crêpes in the produce section of your supermarket. They may be available in several sizes. We tested this recipe using 10-inch crêpes, but determined that any size should work great.

30 MINUTES OR LESS

10-Minute
Bakery-Style Napoleons

We know it's hard, but try not to start drooling all over this page, 'cause this is one recipe you're gonna want to come back to over and over again. After all, who could resist such a pretty pastry-style dessert with layers of creamy filling and decadent frosting? (Certainly not anyone in the Test Kitchen!)

Makes 2

Ingredients

2 (3.25-ounce) store-bought vanilla pudding cups

6 graham cracker sheets

Chocolate frosting (see Tip)

¼ cup confectioners' sugar

1-½ teaspoons water

Preparation

1 Evenly spread 1 container of pudding over 2 graham cracker sheets. Top each with another graham cracker sheet and repeat with another layer of pudding.

2 Spread half the chocolate frosting evenly over the remaining 2 graham cracker sheets and place on top of each stack.

3 In a small bowl, make a glaze by combining confectioners' sugar and water; stir until smooth. Spoon mixture into a resealable plastic bag and using scissors, snip off one corner of bag, making a very small opening. Pipe 4 straight lines lengthwise over each pastry. To create the swirling effect, gently drag a butter knife across the white lines, as shown in the picture.

Note: You can serve these right away, however, we think they're even better when ya let them sit in the fridge for at least an hour or two, so the graham crackers soften up a bit.

Test Kitchen Tip: You can make these with your favorite canned chocolate frosting or you can use our homemade Fudgy Chocolate Frosting on page 228.

30 MINUTES OR LESS

Salted Caramel Apple Crisp

These days everyone from candy manufacturers to trendy dessert boutiques is adding just a little bit of sea salt to their sweet confections to enhance their flavors. When we first tested this combo in our Test Kitchen we knew we had to get on board, too. Of all the ways we tried it, this was one of our favorites. Nothing beats a warm and crumbly apple crisp with a drizzle of salted caramel perfection.

Serves 2

Ingredients

2 tablespoons all-purpose flour, divided

2 tablespoons quick-cooking oats

2 tablespoons light brown sugar

2-½ tablespoons butter, divided

2 apples, cored, peeled, and thinly sliced

1 tablespoon granulated sugar

⅛ teaspoon ground cinnamon

Caramel sauce for drizzling

¼ teaspoon sea salt

Preparation

1 Preheat toaster oven or oven to 375 degrees F. In a small bowl, combine 1 tablespoon flour, the oats, and brown sugar; mix well. Add ½ tablespoon butter and mix until crumbly. Spread mixture onto a foil-lined tray and bake 7 to 8 minutes, or until golden. Set aside.

2 Meanwhile, in a skillet over medium heat, melt remaining 2 tablespoons butter. Add apples, cover, and cook 8 to 10 minutes, or until just tender, stirring occasionally. Stir in granulated sugar, remaining 1 tablespoon flour, and the cinnamon and simmer 1 minute, or until mixture thickens slightly.

3 Spoon apple mixture into 2 dishes, and sprinkle with crumb topping. Drizzle with caramel sauce, sprinkle with sea salt, and serve.

Serving Suggestion: *The best way to enjoy a warm apple crisp is with a big scoop of vanilla ice cream. If ya want, you can also drizzle some of the caramel sauce on it. However you serve this, it's sure to leave you both smiling.*

30 MINUTES OR LESS

Cinnamon-Kissed Poached Pears

Pucker up, 'cause once you get a taste of these cinnamon-kissed pears you're going to want to do some kissing of your own. Whether you choose to kiss the person you're sharing this with or just the recipe page itself is entirely up to you (hey, no judging!). We've gotta warn ya though, cinnamon is known to be quite the aphrodisiac, and it's hard not to fall in love with this dessert.

Makes 2

Ingredients

1 cup apple juice

1 cup water

2 tablespoons cinnamon candies (such as Red Hots)

2 firm pears, peeled and cut in half lengthwise, with seeds removed

2 teaspoons cornstarch

1 tablespoon chopped honey roasted peanuts (see Note)

Preparation

1 In a medium skillet over high heat, bring apple juice, water, and cinnamon candies to a boil. Mix well and add pears. Cover, reduce heat to low, and simmer 15 minutes.

2 Turn pears over and continue cooking 10 to 15 minutes more, or until pears are tender. Using a slotted spoon, remove pears to a plate.

3 In a small bowl, whisk cornstarch and 2 tablespoons of cinnamon liquid. Add cornstarch mixture into skillet and simmer over medium-low heat, whisking constantly. Cook 2 minutes, or until thickened.

4 Cool slightly and spoon sauce over pears. Sprinkle with peanuts and serve.

Note: Most supermarkets carry snack-size packages of peanuts right in the checkout lane, which means you won't have to buy a big can of 'em just to make this recipe.

Serving Suggestion: *These are good whether ya serve 'em hot or cold. And if you want to make these taste even more incredible, just top each with a scoop of vanilla ice cream.*

Giant Dunkin' Chocolate Chip Cookies

Forget sharing your chocolate chip cookies! We've upped the size on this classic cookie so you and your better half can keep your inner cookie monsters smiling and satisfied. Oh, and if you're planning on dunking these, a word of advice, ya may want to fill your soup bowls with milk, since it's going to be pretty hard to find a glass big enough to squeeze these into. Happy dunking!

Makes 2 large cookies

Ingredients

4 tablespoons [½ stick] butter, softened

2 tablespoons light brown sugar

2 tablespoons granulated sugar

1 egg

½ teaspoon vanilla extract

⅔ cup all-purpose flour

½ teaspoon baking soda

⅛ teaspoon salt

⅛ teaspoon ground cinnamon

3 tablespoons dark chocolate chips, divided

Preparation

1 Preheat oven to 350 degrees F. Coat a baking sheet with cooking spray.

2 In a medium bowl, beat together the butter, brown sugar, and granulated sugar until smooth. Add egg and vanilla; mix well. Add flour, baking soda, salt, and cinnamon; mix well. Stir in 2 tablespoons chocolate chips.

3 Divide dough into 2 mounds. Press remaining 1 tablespoon chocolate chips into tops of cookies.

4 Bake 15 to 18 minutes, or until golden. Let cool on baking sheet 10 minutes, then remove to a wire rack to cool completely.

Double-Chocolate Cookies

These cookies are for real chocolate lovers only. We're talking those of you who can really appreciate all the fudgy deliciousness a cookie has to offer, 'cause that's what these are bringing to the table. Unlike other cookies that are either too thin 'n' crispy or too cake-like, these are just perfect. Heads up though: if you find it hard to share these cookies, then you're gonna want to keep 'em tightly sealed. The smell of chocolatey goodness really travels.

Makes 1 dozen

Ingredients

1 cup semisweet chocolate chips, divided

1 (1-ounce) square unsweetened chocolate, chopped

1 tablespoon butter

1 egg, lightly beaten

⅓ cup sugar

2 tablespoons self-rising flour

½ teaspoon vanilla extract

½ cup chopped pecans, toasted

Preparation

1 Preheat oven to 350 degrees F. Coat a baking sheet with cooking spray.

2 In a medium saucepan over low heat, combine ½ cup chocolate chips, the unsweetened chocolate, and butter, stirring until melted. Remove from heat. With a wooden spoon, stir in egg, sugar, flour, and vanilla until combined. Stir in remaining ½ cup chocolate chips and the pecans.

3 Drop by heaping teaspoonfuls, 2 inches apart, onto baking sheet. Bake 10 minutes, or until edges are just set. Remove to a wire rack to cool completely.

Note: If you really love pecans, go ahead and sprinkle some extra on top before baking.

Serving Suggestion: *Once these are cooled, don't waste a second before bagging 'em up, four to a bag, and putting 'em in the freezer. That way, you can have a few on hand for now and have the rest to nibble on over the next week or so. And, since they thaw so quickly, you only have to take them out minutes before ya want 'em.*

30 MINUTES OR LESS

Pineapple Coconut Whip

If you've ever had a pineapple whip at an amusement park or fair stand, then you know that they're sort of a big deal. We love 'em so much we decided to create a version you can make any time you and your sidekick get the hankerin' for something summertime-refreshing.

Serves 2

Ingredients

2 cups frozen pineapple chunks

½ cup coconut milk

1 teaspoon sugar

1 tablespoon toasted coconut

Preparation

1 In a blender or food processor, place pineapple, coconut milk, and sugar. Blend until mixture becomes thick and creamy, stopping once to scrape down sides.

2 Pour into 2 glasses, sprinkle with coconut, and serve immediately.

Mango Peach Whip

When you're looking for a dessert that's lighter in calories and fat, but still big on taste, this is it. With only 195 calories and ½ gram of fat per serving, this is the ideal treat for swimsuit season.

Serves 2

Ingredients

1-½ cups frozen mango chunks

1-½ cups frozen peach slices

¾ cup orange juice

3 tablespoons sugar

Preparation

1 In a blender or food processor, combine all ingredients. Blend until mixture becomes thick and creamy, stopping once to scrape down sides.

2 Pour into 2 glasses and serve immediately.

Serving Suggestions: *We've found that the best way to enjoy these is with a spoon and a straw, so you can get every last drop. And feel free to swap the sugar for a sugar substitute to lighten this up even more.*

30 MINUTES OR LESS

Recipes in Alphabetical Order

Recipes by Category

Recipes by Category

Recipes by Category

Recipes by Category